Gallery Books
*Editor*: Peter Fallon

ONE ANOTHER

for John and Colles Larkin
with compliments
and best wishes —

*Michael Longley*

27 March 2004

St Paul, Minnesota

Michael Coady

# ONE ANOTHER

Gallery Books

*One Another*
is first published
simultaneously in paperback
and in a clothbound edition
on 14 December 2003.

## The Gallery Press
Loughcrew
Oldcastle
County Meath
Ireland

*All rights reserved. For permission
to reprint or broadcast this work,
write to The Gallery Press.*

© Michael Coady 2003

ISBN 1 85235 356 2 (*paperback*)
     1 85235 357 0 (*clothbound*)

A CIP catalogue record for this book
is available from the British Library.

The Gallery Press acknowledges the financial assistance
of An Chomhairle Ealaíon / The Arts Council, Ireland.

# Contents

*for my friend Séamus McGrath*

*But how can time be gathered in and kissed? There is only flesh.*

— John McGahern,
*That They May Face the Rising Sun*

## One Another

*The how or when or where*
*is in the dark or could be*
*closer than the door,*
*but meanwhile as you sit*

*and sip your brandy*
*be assured that all*
*will be taken care of*
*in due course —*

*especially in the light*
*of those men and women*
*just now laughing or*
*contrary at the bar*

*who whenever need arises*
*will not fail to lift and carry*
*you or one another,*
*or to comfort, whenever*

*there are those in need*
*of comforting, just as they*
*themselves will be,*
*eventually.*

*And afterwards, in the*
*accustomed way, there will be*
*a shared remembering*
*that could include of you*

*some things that you yourself*
*may already have forgotten,*
*or never realised,*
*or would prefer unspoken.*

Then, within a month,
that communal recall
must make way for
the beginning of forgetting

for it is remembrance
that allows us
little by little
to forget.

Bleak shelter, this, for
all our nakedness,
but out of it quite suddenly
a surge of unexpected joy

at how you're blessed
amongst those men and women,
one but individual
in their natures at the bar,

all of whom you know
would grant you grace
and do the necessary
for you, just as they'd assume

you'd do for them —
in the ordinary way
that unsung people
just like these

have been easing one another
into all of this and out of it
since this town began
beside the river.

*No need for any song and dance*
*about this commonplace,*
*but keep the moment warm*
*before you say goodnight*

*by calling for another distillation*
*of the sun, the earth,*
*the grape, the time*
*it took, the work*

*of hands, the care,*
*the light of*
*one another*
*in the aftertaste.*

# PART ONE

*Another tide at the bridge of 1447*

*Everything is only for a day, both that which remembers and that which is remembered.*

— Marcus Aurelius, 121-180 AD

## Recycling the Universe

Whenever you rage
at indifferent hands
marring place or form

that touches your heart,
try to be calm, and remember
that much of the given

you see as unspoiled
and true was not
conceived by intent

but shaped by default,
and in the deeper measure of things
is not so long there:

the ancient bridge is only
five centuries made after all,
and the masons were also

thinking of tides and beer
or women and pay
while manhandling stone;

the river itself
did not flow until
the great meltdown

some twelve or so
thousand springs ago,
and even the fabled mountain

of Fionn and the women
had a distant day when it did
not yet stand over the valley.

If you would hold in your hand
some inviolable
nugget of permanence

you could reach down
for any unremarkable
pebble — but then you stand

by a breaking wave and know
that sand between your bare
toes was rock of ages,

just as truly as certain stars
defining the firmament
may already be aeons dark.

Then you might also
recall dustmen
who worked for the Council,

spending their days
walking round the streets
with brushes and shovels —

they won us marks
as a well-kept town, those
men who earned their pay

sweeping up dust
into neat little mounds
that they tidied away.

# The Holes in History

*It takes a great deal of history to produce a little literature.*
— Henry James

Who knows where the crippled
seamstress slept, or what she said,
or ate for breakfast, or what became
of all her stitching?

In the unwritten annals
of the unimportant
we would take account
of the sick child
crying through the night

and of the grooved stone
in the bridge parapet
footnoting whetted knives
of fishermen long dead.

We would research the role
of rain in all our history
and not omit to say
whether the general was intimate
or daggers drawn with his wife
the night before the battle,
and how she coped with toothache —

neither would we discount
as ephemeral asides
the ageless strategies
of dogs and cats, or swans
upon the river on the day
that Cromwell came to visit.

We'd admit as evidence the scrolls
found in the attic of the pub
with their archaeology of whiskies
the boatman downed through years
of turning tides, and how he drowned
before he got to make
a final reckoning

and add the catalogue of measured skulls
at Bourke's clothing emporium
recording headgear preference and fitting
of esquire, priest and merchant —

a meticulous cartography of heads
long since gone to ground
but withheld from the dark
in deathless copperplate.

Along with these neglected sources
showing how it was
we should especially attend

the still unwritten moment
flaring out and
leaping from the tongue

such as last night from Archie Morrissey
prefacing an anecdote with
*I dunno whether this is true or not,*
*but it happened*

or a midnight drinker's
defiant apologia
for farting to the skies —

*It's a sad arse*
*that don't rejoice.*

## Checkpoint

Out of the deep galaxies
of detail and the blind ways
that we go and the light
or dark that shines on us

there is this measure of
the nitty-gritty impact
that I've made so far
upon the earth:

an unreckonable fraction
of a millimetre in
wear-down of polished
kerbstone, the first

on the bridge,
southwestern side,
after I step at half-past
midnight out of

Maggie Dunne's
in Carrick Beg
to cross again
(no record of how many

times in all, of which
no two the same
in one direction
or the other),

cross again that old bridge
built before Columbus,
on my way to sleep
in Carrick Mór

where the weir plays
when the tide's away
and sometimes
between quays

I'm pulled up
and asked where
I've come from
and where I'm going

by stars
that stand
on night-watch
in the river.

## Unstill Life

*with Caltha palustris, Buí Bealtaine, Kingcup,*
*May Blobs, Marsh Marigold*

This given morning of sap-rise
I took my son out fishing on the river.
Instead of trout we brought home flowers

and there they lean voluptuously
together, with glossy petals of deep golden
yellow and dark green leaves and stems
still streaked with river silt

all nested now
in the brown vase
on our living-room table,
reflected in the Victorian wall mirror

that found its way to us
from the landlord's house
above the river —

the mansion that became
a seminary

until vocations to the priesthood
dried and withered,

seeds and seasons infiltrated
doors and windows

and broken floors, staircase
and bedrooms
blossomed.

## Ambush

Hey poet, hey poet,
come here till I tell you
something you never heard.

Jim Quinn is out again, out
of wherever he is when he's in.
People change course,

stepping off the footpath where
he's squatting with his bottle
outside the Bell and Salmon,

hunkered as men once did
in the open to feed or to defecate
or rest from the chase.

We both know the score from of old,
my fingers already sifting
through coins in my pocket.

Hey you sir, he croaks, did you
ever hear tell of a poet by the name of
Rabindranath Tagore in your travels?

Only the wind of the word, I say,
pressing a coin in his hand
as I turn away, when he suddenly

springs from his hunkers
to block my path and declaim
to my face, the street, the world —

*The night is black and the forest has no end;*
*a million people tread it in a million ways.*

*We have trysts to keep in the darkness, but where*
*or with whom — of that we are unaware.*

Are you listenin' to that?
We're inside a dark fucken forest.

What hurry is on you, mister poet?

# Adhlacadh an Dreoilín[1]

*i.m. Michael Hartnett*
*Calvary Cemetery, Newcastle West, 16 October 1999*

You were a wren in your ways and shapes,
king of the birds that could roost in the holly,
land on a leaf or dart to the light,
drop out betimes and go into hiding —

just as now in your tidy nest
you're home and dry though the heavens open
to spill down on our heads and hearts
the clouds' overflow out in Calvary cemetery.

Far from us now the day in John B's
we attempted to rise to *'An Clár Bog Déil'*[2]
on the coat-tails of 'The Limerick Rake',
and Bacchus sporting with Venus.

*I can foretell the past,* you said,
and once, when quizzed by a student at Queen's
about where you stood on religion:
*I'm a catalyst. But I'm a Roman catalyst.*

Little you weigh as they let you down
and you with Ó Bruadair under your belt
along with Haicéad and Ó Rathaille
and all your own hatchings in our two tongues.

When you're tucked away we traipse back to town,
chastened stragglers of the standing army
with west Limerick mud on our soles and uppers,
*agus fágaimid siúd mar atá sé.*[3]

---

[1] The Wren's Burial. [2] The White Deal Board: 18th-century love song.
[3] And let us say no more of that: refrain of ballad 'The Limerick Rake'.

29

## Weathering Angels of Ardmore

They never look up at the round tower,
the weathering angels of Ardmore,
nor out to sea for invaders or friends coming in,
nor do they ever turn aside towards
Michael weighing the souls, or
Adam and Eve about to fall
under the tree nearby that's chiselled in stone.

If you freed your mind for a minute
you might imagine the two of them
gazing out from the heavens some night
and deciding to glide down, making
angelic approach along the Waterford coast
and landing at dawn on the round
tower of Ardmore, for this was a place

they'd heard about, with its saint
whose heaven-sent bell came sailing
over the sea on a floating rock,
and the thousands who gathered each year
on Declan's Day to pray and carouse
and hope for a cure.

A bell tolled noon and from their perch
they saw a crowd wend
out of the village and toil uphill
bearing a human child
to be laid in a hole in the ground
with prayers and reaching of hands
and embracing and tears —

so never again did they spread a celestial
wing except to descend and tenderly
turn to stone, over that freshly made
bed among haphazard cells of clay,

among humps and hollows of time
and memory dressed
in grasses and flowers
breaking from the unfillable
landfill up on the hill

topped by the tower
which men at sea
watch out for
while there's light.

And there they are still, the two
weathering angels of Ardmore,
keeping vigil in a place
where Solomon adjudicates
between the women and the child

a place I like to go
whenever I can if I'm on the road
skirting the coast from Dungarvan to Cork

drawn by unreason to turn
miles out of my way
and touch a fable
of fidelity and pity

now that I've come far enough to know
that reason's a useful thing
to show the way
but only as long
as the light is on.

And there's the heart of the thing —
set aside from the main road,
the elemental grace

and constancy of stone,
marking the mystery
of flesh and blood and bone

for it comforts me always to know
of the angels there in winter dusk
with all below in the village engrossed
in a clamorous box of shadows,
their windows double-glazed against
whatever may come.

Under all seasons
the weathering angels stand
with eyes cast down,
reflecting on innocent earth

telling all I can't hear,
showing all I can't see,
waiting for what I don't know

through ordinary hours
or dazzling noons,
mimed nocturnes of moonlight,
manic symphonies of storm,

on the honeycombed hill
with the finger of stone
that points to the dark and the stars
above land and sea in Ardmore.

# PART TWO

*Wind of the Word*

*Frosty weather,*
*Snowy weather,*
*When the wind blows*
*We all go together.*
                    — Children's rhyme

# Good Friday Bread

In the hard times the nuns started a little laundry at the convent down in the Well Road and the women around there used to work in it. For some it was all they had to live on and a godsend. Though the wages were small they used to get their dinner as well, and their tea before they went home in the evenings.

Nell Delaney had a houseful of children that were under-nourished. Her husband used to work loading and unloading barges for the grain merchant down on the quay. Twenty-stone sacks in all weathers with no mercy or let up. Those men were treated like beasts of burden.

After a fall he was let go and had to mind the youngsters while Nell went out to the laundry. And when it came to the meals at the convent she used to stow away some of the food about her person, and often leave herself hungry. She'd hide as much as she could in her clothes and under her shawl to bring home to the children.

Some of the other women used to mock her about it. They used to make little of the misfortunate woman for being so badly off.

Every Good Friday work would stop in the laundry before three o'clock and all the women would go to the convent chapel along with the nuns. When Nell Delaney's turn came to kiss the cross she walked up the aisle of the church and bent down over the crucifix that was laid out on the altar steps, and all the bread she had hidden inside her bosom tumbled out at the feet of Jesus.

# The Via Roma

It took three different buses to get to Glanmire when I heard Paddy was bad. Are you a relation? the nurse asked.

A relation? I said. Weren't our fathers and mothers living over-right one another in Sir John's Road? Aren't we hunting rabbits together above in the Gap of Rathclarish since we were boys? And didn't the two of us hurl with the Kickhams?

I hardly knew him in the bed. And people all around him as bad, or worse. Lining out for the bone-yard. Well Paddy, I said. You're coming around bit by bit. You won't know yourself when you get out of here.

Won't know myself is right, said Paddy. How's Rosie?

His Jack Russell bitch. He left her with me when he had to go in for the operation. Rosie is grand, I said. I'm minding her. I needn't tell you half the country is calling in night noon and morning asking to breed pups off her.

Have nothing to do with them, said Paddy. None of them has a dog could hold a candle to her. Men used to come to me from even beyond Thurles. Do you remember all the great days above in the Gap, with that lurcher you used to have? Hobo. Heading off on a Sunday morning after seven Mass on the two bikes. Rosie sitting up on the little rest I made for the crossbar. And the ferret in the box across my shoulder.

And Hobo trotting along behind, I said. And boiling up the black gallon for the tea when we'd stop around the middle of the day above the woods of Ballinurra to give the dogs a rest from the hunting. We'll have them days again.

We won't, said Paddy. I'm finished. I was thinking last night about the big singsongs we used to have in Mikey Gavin's of a Monday night. Will you sing a verse of 'The Via Roma' for me, Stevie?

I dunno when I sang that song last, I said. The days of the big nights is gone. I'm only after getting over a bit of a chest infection. Would the rest of them mind a bit of singing here? Would they object, like?

Mind me arse, said Paddy. They never heard a decent singer in this place. Give us 'The Via Roma', Stevie. It would be as good as a tonic for me.

So I cleared my chest out a bit and started singing, and all of a sudden everything stopped in its tracks. Nurses and all came in and stood there without a stir out of them, and two doctors in white coats. I gave the whole song and I didn't hold anything back in the voice. When I was finished they were full of *plámás*\* and bringing us in tea and toast.

You never lost it, Stevie, said Paddy.

The next time we met up he was coming home in a box.

\*soft talk

# Happening

This is only supposed to be happening since they did up the place. I never heard any talk of it in the time of the old pub. And I never saw them myself until last Sunday night. But I know several others who were after seeing them before that, and were talking about it on the quiet. As if they were half-afraid even to mention it to one another.

A man and a woman, more than middle-aged and dressed in an old-fashioned way. The kind of people you'd see in the old days, maybe in from the butt of the Comeraghs to do some necessary business in the town. A man and his wife probably, the two of them in dark clothes. You know the way certain married couples get to look like brother and sister? As if they were always together and there was never a time they didn't know one another or live in the same house.

If Marion is after seeing them from behind the bar she never mentioned it to anyone, and no one mentioned it to her. She could take the nose off you, so you'd rather not risk upsetting her. You could just imagine her spitting back at you about ould *pisreogs** and bad-minded people trying to frighten customers away. It could be she's blind to it all, or she might know already but be staying quiet about it. Maybe she should have a Mass said in the place. But that would be certain to draw the talk of the whole town if it got out.

You can only look at them out of the corner of your eye. Or so I heard from some in the know. Look straight at them and they're gone. And Jesus I have to admit that last Sunday night I felt the hair rising on the back of my neck. They're here, I said to myself with a shock. They're here. I was sitting up on a stool at the far end of the bar. And just as I raised my eyes from my drink I spotted them coming in through the solid wall and passing through the customers who were drinking and talking and watching the match on the television.

They were just like two quiet country people going to the end of the room and sitting down. Sitting there, not even looking at each other. But a bit stooped and pale, the two of them, a bit

*superstitions

weighed down, as if there was something troubling them. There used to be a door where they came in through the wall, and where they sat down there was a fireplace long ago but it was filled in and plastered over.

Maybe something happened in the place that we don't know about. Something in the past. But sure didn't things happen every place that we don't know about? Isn't every room and house and street in the town full of invisible happenings if it comes to that? Like that high wall just around the corner from the pub, leading up the steep hill and bounding the old church and the graveyard. That wall was built to give work to starving people during the Famine. Every stone of it must carry a story you'd be better off not knowing.

# The Saint's Instructions

When the knock came to the door that morning there was no one else in the house with me except my older brother Bob. I was around ten at the time. The two of us should have been getting ready for school. My mother was off out working at Hurley's farm in Glen, and she'd be gone before six to walk the five miles out.

Anyway there was Peter Woods at the door when Bob opened it. Peter had a bit of land. He owned a few fields at the butt of Carrick Beg Hill and he lived in Gorey Lane. I say a prayer for him every night.

Get ready, he said to Bob. I want to bring the two of ye across the town. A saint appeared to me last night in a dream and he gave me instructions. You know them two boys belonging to Mrs Power near the chapel gate? he said to me. That poor woman is hard up since Bill died sudden on St Brigid's Day.

Peter was right about that. It was the first day of the salmon season and my father had everything in order; the cot tied below at the slip, with the net and paddles all ready in it. He was waiting for the start of the floodtide. Then he got a bit of a pain across his chest and in five minutes he was gone. He never got to wet a paddle or a net before slipping off into eternity.

Let the two of ye hurry up now, said Peter. I'm under orders. Go across to that house first thing in the morning and bring them two boys over the town, the saint said to me. Put proper clothes and shoes on them.

And that's what happened. He followed the saint's instructions. He led myself and Bob across the Old Bridge, up to the Main Street and into Morrissey's the drapers. I want you to outfit them two boys from head to foot, he said to Willie Morrissey. Vests and shirts and suits and socks. Overcoats as well. Whatever they need.

Then he brought us across the street to Meany's for new boots. That was old John Meany, father of Dick. Now, he said, here's a half-crown each and another for your mother. Tell her I'm going on the saint's instructions. And I won't forget ye for the future.

It was nearly dark when my mother got back from the farm in

Glen, with a gallon of new milk. She couldn't get over what happened, and Bob and I didn't know what to do with ourselves in all them new clothes. Over to Peter Woods straight away to thank him. You're too good to us, my mother said, and here's a sup of new milk for you.

It wasn't me at all, said Peter. It was the saint that came to me last night. I'll be leaving ye a field in my will as well.

But he never put that down in writing and maybe we were better off without it.

# Nightdress

I have looked into the depths.

Where did I hear that first? Or did I dream it or make it up? I say it to myself now and there's some kind of cure buried in it, though the wound can never be healed. As though we're after becoming a part of some great mystery. Something deeper than we ever thought existed.

I used to bring the little nightdress to bed with me every night for a good while. Tuck it under my pillow or drape it around my neck. I never washed it. Because her scent was still on it. Poor Jimmy beside me. Our hearts broken after the year of going to the hospital, with hope draining away week by week, though we tried to give faith to one another.

You'd have this awful need to explain to her how sorry you were that this happened to her and how much you loved and treasured her. You wanted to hold her and rock her to sleep in your arms. What could you explain about life and death to a child only going on four?

It would leave you demented. As though you were somehow to blame because she looked up to you to cure everything, even if it was only a little scratch on her knee when she fell in the garden. As if you let her down by not being able to make her better. If you could, you'd go to the ends of the earth to do it. The ends of the earth.

Neighbours at their wits' end wondering what else they could do for us. You wouldn't know what to say to them. How could you explain that it wasn't us that mattered? We'd have to carry whatever we had to carry. What mattered was to comfort the child. And that was beyond us all.

It was private and public. Hoping people weren't noticing how we were constantly going to the grave and talking to her. As quietly as we could. Apologising to her for having to leave her there. And breathing in her scent, for as long as it lasted, from the nightdress I held close to me in bed. Using it to wipe away tears.

How many times did this happen before in this town? And everywhere. Beginning with a man and woman making love, and having a child. And losing the child. I never thought of them before. All the demented parents. People we never heard of. The names and stories lost and forgotten. But going through the same thing as ourselves in their time.

And yes, it'll be all the same in a hundred years, or even in fifty. But saying that makes no difference, no difference at all. It's just a thing we all say, for want of something to say. In a hundred years there'll be others, just like us.

Poor Jimmy beside me, lying there like a stone. A hundred years gone by or still to come means nothing to him. This minute is all that matters. I'm trying to persuade him to take down the fishing rod again. You can't stay turned into yourself I tell him. You have to get out from under it. You have to open the door, go out for the paper and look up the horses. Or down to the river to try a few casts.

I say it now to help put myself to sleep. I have looked into the depths.

# Midwinter Butterfly

Because I was after making my First Communion that year, my father brought me to Midnight Mass and up to the choir in the gallery where the organ is. From the church porch you have to go up this narrow stairs with two turns in it, so steep it's a bit like going up a ladder, with a railing to hold on to. And when you get to the top and come out on a kind of balcony you see all the people below, and the altar way off at the top of the church, and the crib over to the side, and all the lights and candles and flowers, and the Christmas tree on the other side.

The organ is just behind your back, with pipes going up to the roof. The big ones are for the low down notes. And a man plays it with his hands and feet at the same time. His name is Michael. While he's playing he has his back to everyone so he has to have a mirror up in front of him to see what's going on down in the church. And a special lamp so he can see the music. Some of the old people in the choir find it hard getting up the steep stairs.

The oldest woman's name is Eily. She was out of breath for a few minutes after getting there. Then she asked me my name and my age. James, she said. And you're only eight. Well imagine this, if you know your tables. I'm ten times older than you. I used to know your father's grandfather. I remember him conducting the band at the regatta long ago when I was a girl. It's nearly time I packed it in.

When the choir started to sing with the organ you could feel the floorboards vibrating under your feet. It was like the whole building was turned into music. Way down in the church I could see my mother, with Lucy and Niamh. It took me a while to spot where they were. The whole place was packed, with some people standing at the sides.

I was joining in with some of the easy carols, such as 'Away in a Manger', but other times the men and women were all singing different notes at the same time called harmony, with the choirmaster whose name is Nicholas conducting them. Dad sings the low notes. They call it the bass. Some of the choir make kind of funny faces and mouths while they're singing.

In the middle of it I looked up towards the roof of the church and then behind me at the big organ pipes that were playing.

And suddenly a butterfly flew out of the pipes high up. He fluttered around in the light, then down across the empty space over all the people. I don't know how many saw him. Then he flew back up to the choir and before I knew what was happening he landed straight on top of my head and took a rest there for a minute.

I didn't know what to do but I could feel myself blushing up to my hair. I looked up at Dad but his head was stuck in the music because they were all singing a big harmony chorus of fall on your knees, oh hear the angel voices.

The old woman Eily was looking over at me though, and she saw what happened. Her eyebrows went up above her glasses and she sort of smiled even though she was still singing. When it was all over she said to me, James, you'll remember this night. I don't know where that butterfly came out of. He must have been dreaming up there behind the organ since the summer.

# PART THREE

A GRAND

# DANCE

WILL BE HELD IN

# THE HALL,

BALLYHALE

ON

# ST. STEPHEN'S NIGHT,

DECEMBER 26th, 1937.

MUSIC BY

Miss Doreen Power's Dance Band

(WATERFORD)

Dancing at 9 p.m. to 4 a.m.

*Braithim brí na ndeor is na bpóg:*
*ní chailltí daoine nuair a bhíos óg.*
I understand the meaning of tears and kisses:
no one died when I was young.

— Michael Hartnett,
'Mé Féin'/'Portrait'

# The Friction of Feet in Time

Once upon those nights
with Joe Carroll on trumpet
Jack Doherty on bass
and my mother Dora on piano

with myself at seventeen on trombone
and Davy Heffernan beating time
on bass drum and brushed calfskin . . .

Once upon some little hall located
along byroads difficult to find

before the broken lid
is closed on the piano
and the band packed for the road

before the person with the key
turns out the lights
on dusty creak and scented
sigh of absence

my uncle Peter lays aside the sax to sing
    *Goodnight sweetheart*
    *Till we meet tomorrow*

over heads of men and women moving
anti-clockwise in their holding
of each other and the moment
and the music that embraced them.

Once upon those nights
if you stood outside the hall
you could hear inside

the shuffling unanimity
of feet in time

like a grounded being
moving underneath the music
in a relentless drag and slide —

*shoo    shoo*
*shoo-sha shoo*
*shoo-sha    shoo*
*shoo-sha shoo-sha*

That against the gravity of darkness
over and around a little hall
past byroads difficult to find

once upon those nights of
*shoo    shoo    shoo-sha shoo*

once    once    once upon
    once    once    once upon
        once    once    once upon

# The Company of Absence

*i.m. Paddy Clancy, actor and singer, 1922-1998*

The night he was taken to the chapel
there was so loud a gathering
of rounds and grief and laughter
where he used to drink

that they never heard
the gale of wind and rain
that tried all doors and windows
but had passed on down the valley

by the time befuddled heads
turned out into
the street of the small hours
to find their pillows,

leaving him alone up there
to lie in the big silence,
this one and only night
of all his nights, with less

and more of company
than he'd ever known,
before the altar
and the tabernacle

under the high
reach of roof
and generations
in the dark.

## Two Close Encounters

James Joyce,
impersonating a Franciscan
at Mass in Carrick Beg,

glaring through thick glasses,
as he holds up the Host
before each communicant
with a singsong

*Bawdy of Christ,*
*Bawdy of Christ,*
*Bawdy of Christ.*

Samuel Beckett thinly
disguised as a sergeant from Thomastown
suddenly appearing
in the midst of late-night men
at Power's of Tullahought,

laying on the existential lash with

*What kind of an hour is this?*

## Le Jazz Hot

The first time I met up
at the age of sixteen
with the real live thing

I knew it at once —
that unfettered outcry
extemporising joy

and swinging
with such casual precision,
like a riff I recognised

from a past
I hadn't had
but was about to begin.

That first night
when all of me flushed yes
to ravishing surprise

a shameless grace
stepped out
of its clothes

without missing
a single breath
or beat

and danced in its skin
saying come
on in.

# Seventh Position

*(in which the trombone slide is fully extended and the player's arm at full stretch)*

My uncle's elbow rose again
when they opened the family

grave to bury my mother,
but the bone held back and hid

just under the surface
until a night of steady rain

revealed it just in time to coincide
with her Month's Mind —

and that's how I came to meet him again,
after all the years since he drew last breath

while playing at a dance one night
when I was going on twenty.

Before I found a spade to return
the bone discreetly to its place

I remembered how he always swore
by Ponds Cold Cream

as the one and only lubricant
for the slide trombone, and I felt

the ineffable lightness now of all
I held in my hand, and the flowing

mystery of all the times he bent
his elbow at bars beyond counting

or tenderly over the tousled heads
of his dreaming children

or in embracing Katie his wife
in their waking or sleeping

or repainting Main Street shops for little money
before the Corpus Christi procession

or papering the town's eccentric rooms
and ceilings that never knew right angles

or upfront in the brass band, storming
through the West Gate with the bass

chorus of 'Old Comrades' causing doors
and windows to tremble with its passing,

or off by night in dance halls
with the Riverside Swingsters,

uncorking dark bottles between sets
and swearing over missed notes

and tricky slide-work in the turn
of 'Anything Goes'

or the ride-out chorus of
'That's A-Plenty'.

*World-losers and world-forsakers*
*On whom the pale moon gleams.*

## Cold Feet

The usual hole
in the ground

on another bitter
day that could

give you
your death

if you stood
too long around —

but fair play to you
Frank, as we bless

ourselves and turn
on our heels

we have to allow
that you were

the best man
ever to dance

the tango
in this town.

# An Updated History of Sexual Intercourse

*Love is eternal for as long as it lasts.*
> — Vinícius de Morais

All those ancestral hots that brought
us here — nakedness and faces,
hearts and times and places,

and intimate occasions
way beyond our knowing,
with ins and outs uncountable

by fields of folk who
pair by pair and real
in their skin

knew impassioned
throes of pant and thrust
towards the unreachable

back of the cave, the grail,
the unappeased desire of all
flesh for some final

reach and touch
across the sweet divide
of man and woman

some shudder that might fuse
our human brokenness
forever, conceivably

in chaos theory triggering
a cosmic chain reaction,
a beatific big-bang

consummation of all
consummations that might
once and for all

at long and last
resolve absolutely
everything.

Meanwhile in the carnal war
with time that's always lost
but never conceded

the front line forever changes
but remains the same
in its unclothed strategy

of love and lust
and little death attending
the brief blind rapture

designed to pass it on
(whatever it is)
for others to pass on.

I'm talking
*humanae vitae*
here, for it's

as simple and sweet
and deep as that,
my dear,

with a hey
and a ho
and hallelujah

before the lay me
down to sleep,
before the night,

the dark,
the dream,
before the lone,

before the lone,
before the lone-
some valley.

# Twenty-four Hours from Tulla

Stopping for a leak in the County Limerick
suddenly I slip into the deep of the world,
after midnight and the stars upstanding,
engine idling and radio on, with Pavarotti
sending *E lucevan le stelle*\*
up into the night and out across
blind fields where distantly
a beast is bellowing some distress.

I too am in the dark
as I piss into a ditch
to an aria from *Tosca*,
just over the threshold
of the thirteenth of October
in the year two thousand —
Pavarotti's birthday, the presenter said,

and also, as it happens, a poet's
anniversary: a year to the day
since, peeling potatoes at the sink,
I was ambushed by the news
of Michael Hartnett's passing,
itemized before the latest
update on the weather.

But *bravo*, Luciano, *bravo!*
Wherever you are I'm sure
candles are alight, corks
popping, music swelling for
your sixty-fifth live
lap around the sun.

\*the stars were shining

Meanwhile, back in Newcastle West,
my greetings to you, Michael,
after your first solar circuit
under sod in Calvary Cemetery
where all are teetotallers
and no one complains.

I don't miss chats we never had
about poetics or postmodernism
whenever our paths crossed, but that
running ad lib game we made
of relocating songs —

I want to be a part of it —
New Ross, New Ross!
you might insist,

while I'd respond with Kilfenora,
where the wind comes sweeping down the plains
and one could meet a *spéir-bhean**

tall and tan and young and lovely,
the Girl from Inchigeelagh,
lost and lonely in the Burren.

Be sure of this, you'd say,
if I was there she'd sidle up
beside me at the bar

and sing into my ear —
Fly me to Macroom
and let me play among the stars.

*a beauty

64

How little I know, Michael,
in this here and now, and what
I think I understand reduces day by day
as though I gravitate towards
a baseline of unknowing
that may (for all I know)
be bliss.

*E lucevan le stelle.*
In what townland am I standing?
Tell me the name of that star up there —
no, not the bright one
but the fainter one behind it
(*behind* it?).

Anyway, what's in a name,
and who do I think I'm asking?
Dark or day it's always
someone's birthday
or the birthday of their death.
So all together now —
Michael, myself, Sinatra,
Puccini, Luciano —

*Fill my heart with song
and let me sing forevermore.*

# PART FOUR

*lingo@Acts2:6-12*

Sníomna.

añroiɲ añ a   6 Agur a ɲoul oón tárgɾo amaċ
ɲa, eaoon, oo ċɾuiñiȝ an cóiṁtionól. agur oo
           báoa buaioeɲta, oo bɾiȝ ȝo ȝcúal-
a léabɾa na ɾó, ȝaċ áon aca iaoɾan aȝ lábaiɲt
ṁ̇iɲɾoe na añ a oteɲȝɾó féiɲ.
oiɲe a bɾt   7 Agur oo ȝáb úatbar 7 ioɲȝ-
le a ȝɾbóȝ- aɲtar iao vle, aȝ ɾáo ɲé céile,
           Féuċ, a ɲé ɲaċ Ȝaiɲleeaɲvȝ iaoɾo
éiȝiɲ áon vle lábɾar?
on ɾiñe a   8 Agur cioñar oo clvɲ ɾiñe ȝaċ
a ɲoȝcaɾo áon aȝvn a oteɲȝɾó féiɲ, añ a ɾuȝao
ɾur amaċ iñ?
           9 Páti, 7 Ṁéoi, 7 elamiti, 7 na
ȝɾo Eóiɲ, oáoiɲe áitiȝer a Ṁeropotáɲia, 7 a
vuar uáiɲ ɲIúoéa, 7 a ȝCappaoócia, a bPoɲe-
aiɲɲe na uɾ, 7 añ ɾa ɲAɾia,
           10 A bPɾiȝia, 7 bPampilia, añ ɾa
r, Ióɾeɲ, ɲeȝipt, 7 a ɾañtɾb Libia timċeall
cóṁaiɲm Chɾéɲe, 7 coiȝcɾioċta na Róṁa, 7
ȝe oóib,    Iúoɾoe 7 Pɾoreliti,
           11 Luċo Chɾéta aȝur Aɾábia,
iȝeɲɲa, oo clvɲmio iao aȝ lábaiɲt añ aɲ
ȝáoiɲe], oteɲȝtɾb féiɲ oibɾeċa móɲoálaċa
ȝ tú.   Dé.
           12 Agur oo ȝáb úatbar, 7 aṁgar
ɾa, ó a iao vle, aȝ ɾáo ȝaċ feɲ ɲé a céile,
ɾur ȝo Cɾéuo ir ciall oó ɾo!
           13 Agur a ɾú...

*All things counter, original, spare, strange.*

— Gerard Manley Hopkins,
'Pied Beauty'

# The Gift of Tongues

In his own way he was gifted, and that's gospel. From the time he was confirmed he could put talk on all classes, creeds and colours.

And they'd all understand him. People from Joanstown, Garravoone, Ballyknock, Ballindesert, Killballyquilty, Rathgormack and Ballyhest. From Feddans, Coolnahorna, Killerguile, Moonaminaun, Ballyvalikan, Glenaphooka, Curraghballintlea or Portnaboe. Awkward customers or harmless people in from Crehana, Tinhalla, Brownswood, Coolfin, Ballynab, Fews, Monadiha, Sheskin, Coolnamuck or as far away as Kyledroughtaun.

Across the river the same story. He could fluently converse with people living in and around Ballinderry, Mullagh, Ballinagrana, Baungarrif, Garrynarea, Knockroe, Killonerry and Knocknaconnery. Total strangers and able dealers from out beyond the borders of Glenbower, Macreary, Lisadobber, Cloghapistol, Poulmoleen, Skough, Tullahought, Ahenny, Rathclarish, or Tibberaghny. He could talk to them all, and often the less he said the more they took it to mean.

Of course he was travelled. Matches and funerals all over the county. And pilgrimages further afield. And weddings when he was asked, which was seldom. No bother at all to him to *plámás* his way around women from here to Donegal. Each one would hear whatever she wanted to hear. Didn't he head off once on a skite with a nun back from the missions that he met up with in Lough Derg? His way of living was a bit of a mystery. Fixing up bikes and radios on the side, and televisions in the days of black and white. He could tell straight away what was up with the gears or the sound or vision; whether it was curable or beyond redemption.

But mostly he talked his way through the world. Married, yes. A small woman that came from Kilkenny as housekeeper in the Friary. Perpetual Succour she was called behind her back. She had the measure of him if anyone did. But hardly ever opened her mouth in public, except for novenas and hymns.

God knows how they ever got on in the house. Or the feathers. She could reach into the bosom for the deadly weapon of silence. They met first when she walked by him one evening out in Dead

Man's Boreen. A certain look she gave him going past. Or so he's supposed to have admitted in drink to a man who asked his advice on how to go about meeting a wife.

Of course you could only put up with him in small doses. Eventually barred from every pub and bookie's shop in the town on account of all the smart talk and the ructions and rear-ups that could break out in five minutes. You still can't even mention his name within earshot of certain individuals; mostly contrary hoors themselves. Bring up the name and they'll start to froth at the mouth. Maybe recalling card games that ended in mayhem. Or times they knew they were being highly insulted, even though he might only raise an eyebrow and say 'Hmmm?' in a certain way.

Ten years on his back in the Friary graveyard without a geek out of him, but still all the stories about him and what he's supposed to have said. He might as well still be around.

# Bua na Cainte

*Version in the Irish of Ring, Co Waterford, by Áine Uí Fhoghlú*

Tabhairse an leabhar go raibh a bhua neamhchoitianta fhéin aige. Ón uair a chuaigh sé fé láimh an easpaig, gheobhadh sé caint a chur ar shlua Mhurchaidh is ar shluaite nach iad.

Agus thuigidís go léir é. Ó Bhaile Shiobhán, Garbh Mhóin, Baile an Chnoic, Baile an Dísirt, Cill Bhaile Uí Chaoilte, Ráth Ó gCormaic agus Baile hEist. Muintir na bhFeadán, Cúl na hEornan, Cill ar gCoill, Móin Mionáin, Baile Bhailicín, Gleann a' Phúca, Currach Bhaile an tSléibhe nó Port Úth na Bó. Daoine ciotacha nó ainniseoirí neamhdhíobhálacha a thiocfadh isteach ó Chriothánach, Tigh an Chalaidh, Coill a' Bhrúnaigh, Cúil Fhinn, Baile an Abadh, na Feadha, Móin na Daibhche, Seisceann, Cúl na Muice, nó chomh fada ó bhaile le Cill Drúchtáin.

Ba mhar a chéile an scéal aige é ar an mbruach thall. Dhéanfadh sé comhrá líofa le háitreathóirí Bhealach an Doire, Mullach, Baile na gCránach, an Bán Garbh, Garraí na Réithe, Cnoc Rua, Cill Ó Neire, Cnoc na Conaire agus na bailte máguaird. Fearaibh aniar nó mangairí cumasacha aduaidh thar teorainn ó Ghleann Bodhar, Magh Criathrach, Lios a' dTobair, Cloch a' Phiostoil, Poll Moilín, An Sceach, Tulchacht, Áth Eine, Ráth Chláiris nó Tiobra Fhachtna. Gheobhadh sé caint a chur ar gach éinne riamh acu, agus dá laghad a dheireadh sé babhtaí, 'sea is mó brí a shíleadar a bhí ag baint leis.

Dar ndóigh bhí cuid mhór dhen saol curtha de aige, gach cluiche agus sochraid dá raibh sa chontae. Agus níos sia ó bhaile ná san. Bainiseacha fiú, cé nach ró-mhinic a gheibheadh sé cuireadh chucu san. Ní chuirfeadh sé mairg sa saol air mná a phlámás is a bhladar as so go Dún na nGall. Dh'aireodh gach bean acu pé rud ba mhaith léi fhéin a dh'aireachtaint uaidh. Nár dh'imigh sé de scít, uair, le bean rialta a bhí tar éis casadh ós na misiúin, ar theagmhaigh sé léi thuas i Loch Dergdherc? Saghas rúndiamhar ba dh'ea an tslí bheatha a bhí aige. Dheisíodh sé rothair is craolacháin nuair a bheadh sé dh'uain aige agus na seana theilifíseanna fadó fé'r tháinig an dath. Dhearbhódh sé dhuit láithreach cad a bhí bun os cionn leis na gear-anna nó leis a' bhfuaim nó leis an bpeictiúr, nó an bhfaighfí é a réiteach nó an raibh sé thar cumas.

Ach ba dh'í an chaint a b'fhearr leis lena shaol. Sea, bhí sé pósta, leis. Binnín bheag a tháinig anoir ó Chill Chainnigh mar bhean tí sa bhFriary. Máthair na Buanchabhrach a thugaidís uirthi i ngan fhios. Má bhí sé tomhaiste go maith 'ge éinne, is aici sin a bhí. Ach b'annamh léi labhairt i measc na ndaoine seachas nuair a bhíodh nóibhíne nó iomainn le rá.

N'fheadar éinne nach Dia conast mar a réitíodar sa tigh. Ná sa tocht. Gheobhadh sí an ciúnas marfach a tharraingt chuici dá mba dhóigh léi gur ghá é. Ar Bhóithrín an Fhir Mhairbh a theagmhaíodar lena chéile tráthnóna amháin don chéad uair riamh. Pé féachaint a thug sí air agus í ag góilt thairis. Nó sin é mar a deirtear a dh'admhaigh sé agus an braon istigh aige nuair a dh'iarr fear a chomhairle maidir le bean a dh'fháilt do fhéin.

Ach, dar ndóigh ní ró-fhada a dh'fhoighneofá riamh é. Níorbh fhada gur thug gach tábhairneoir agus geallghlacadóir ar an mbaile an bóthar do de dheasca a chabaireacht ghasta ghlic, gan trácht ar an gcibeal agus an scliúchas a gheobhadh briseadh amach tar éis chúig númant ar an láthair. Gheobhadh sé a bheith baolach fós a ainm a lua i ngoirracht scread asail do dhaoine áirithe; cuid acu san fhéin ina gcancráin, cruthanta ceart. A ainm a tharraingt anuas, fiú, agus bheadh cúr conaidh leo. Iad ag cuimhneamh, b'fhéidir, ar chluichí cártaí a mbíodh marú mar chríoch leo. Nó ar uaireanta eile nuair a thuigidís go raibh an masla go smior á thabhairt aige cé ná déanfadh sé ach mala a dh'árdach in slí ar leith agus crónán éigint do-thuigthe a scaoileadh uaidh.

Deich mbliana anois athá sé sínte gan gíocs as i gcré na cille sa bhFriary agus fós thá trácht agus seanchas air fhéin agus a chuid eachtraí. Bheadh sé chomh maith aige bheith fós inár measc.

# The Gift o Tongues

*Version in Ulster-Scots by James Fenton, Co Antrim*

In his ain wie he wuz gifted an that's the Guid's truth. Frae the confirmin he could crak wae a' kines, creeds an colours.

An they'd ivery yin untherstan him. Yins frae Joanstown, Gairravoone, Bellyknock, Bellindesert, Killybellyquulty, Rathgormack an Bellyhest. Frae Faeddans, Coolnahoarna, Killerguile, Moonaminaun, Bellyvalikan, Glenaphooka, Curraghbellintlea or Portnaboe. Akward clients or hairmless yins in frae Crehana, Tinhalla, Broonswud, Coolfin, Bellynab, Fews, Monadiha, Sheskin, Coolnamuck or as far awa as Kyledroughtaun.

The ither side o the watther the yin story. He could lee it aff lake thon tae yins leevin in or aboot Bellinderry, Mullagh, Bellinagrana, Baungarrif, Garrynarea, Knockroe, Killonerry an Knocknaconthery. Oot-an-oot sthrangers an able dailers frae oot ayont the bordhers o Glenboor, Macreary, Lisadabber, Cloghapistol, Poulmoleen, Skough, Tullahought, Ahenny, Rathclerish or Tibberaghny. He could crak wae them a', an gye affen the less he allooed the mair they taen ooty it.

O coorse he had been aroon. Fitba matches an funtherals a' ower the county. An thraiks awa beyont that. An waddins, gin he wuz aksed, whutch wuznae affen. Nae bother ava tae him tae weegle an work his wie roon weemen frae this tae Dinnygaal. Ivery yin wud hear whutiver she wuz luckin tae hear. Dint he tak off yince on a kerrant wae a nun hame frae the missions he run inty in Lough Derg? His wie o leevin wuz a weethin o a puzzler. Squarin bikes an wirelesses amang hans, an tellyveesions in the dehs o blak an white. He could speer sthrecht awa whut wuz the metther wae the geers or the soon or veesion; whather it micht be soarted or wuz lang by daein ocht wae.

But moistly he talked his wie through the worl. Married, aye. A wee wumman that come frae Kilkenny as hoosekeeper in the Friary. Perpaityal Succour she wuz ca'd ahint hir bak. Thon hizzy had the misure o him if oanyboady did. But harly iver appened hir mooth ootby, ither nor for the novena prayin an hymns.

Guid knows hoo they iver pulled at hame. Or unther the

73

quult. She hel aye tae yin deedly waipon: nae crakkin. Their furst encoonther wuz whun she gaen by him yin evenin oot in Deed Man's Rodden. A kine o a gleek she taen at him gan by. Or sae he should'a gien inty wae the drink on him, tae a boady luckin his advice on finnin a wumman.

O coorse ye could only hae him a wee lock at the time. At the hinther en barred frae ivery pub an bookie's shap in the toon on acoont o his owl smairt tak an the hurries an thrades wud brek oot lake thon. Tae noo there's a wheen o boys ye darnae name him afore; moistly conthrairy hoors theirsels. Jaist dhrappin the name'll gar them froathe at the mooth. Aiblins minin caird games wud'a ent in a whurang. Or whiles they'd jalooze weel enugh the heech wie he wuz leein yin inty them, the mair he micht jaist rise an eebroo and gie a 'Hmmm?' thon wie.

Ten year on the braid o his bak in the Friary graveyaird and naw a myowt ooty him, but yit wae a' the tellures aboot him an whut he should'a said. He micht as weel be aboot yit.

# Am Beul-Bòidheach

*Version in Scots Gaelic by Rody Gorman, Isle Ornsay, Isle of Skye*

Abair bodach ealanta — 's e 'n fhìrinn a th' agam! Riamh o bha e
na bhalach, bhruidhneadh e ris a h-uile mac màthar is nighean
athar.

Agus bhiodh iad ga thuigsinn. An fheadhainn anns an Aird is
ann an Capasdail 's ann an Camard 's ann an Tòrr Mòr 's ann an
Caileagarraidh 's ann an Aird a' Bhàsair 's ann an Armadail. Ann
an Ostaig 's anns a' Chille Mhòir 's anns a' Chille Bhig 's ann am
Fearann Dòmhnaill 's anns an Teanga 's ann an Sàsaig 's ann an
Tòrabhaig 's ann an Duisdeil 's ann an Eilean Iarmain. Bodaich is
cailleachan is ceàrdan 's ceannaichean, daoine garbh is daoine gun
lochd ann an Camas Chros 's air a' Chruard 's ann am Barabhaig
's ann an Ceannloch is anns an Druim Fheàrna 's ann an Sgulamas
's ann am Breacais is ann an Aiseag no cho fad' air falbh ri Caol
Reatha.

An aon rud thall air tìr-mòr. Bhruidhneadh e cho fileanta ri
bàird ris an fheadhainn ann an Caol Loch Aillse 's ann an
Earbarsaig 's ann an Diùirinis is anns a' Phloc 's anns an Achadh
Mhòr 's anns an t-Sròm 's ann an Atadal 's ann an Srath Carrann.
Daoine ris nach do thachair e riamh is a nochdadh far nan
crìochan ann am Baile Mac Ara 's air an Dòirnidh 's ann an Cinn
Tàile 's ann an Innis a' Chrò 's ann an Gleann Seile 's ann an
Ràtagan 's ann an Leitir Feàrna 's ann an Gleann Eilg 's ann an
Arnasdal 's anns a' Chorran. Bhruidhneadh e ris a h-uile mac aon
dhiubh agus gu tric mar bu lugha chanadh e fhèin 's ann a bu
mhotha de bhrìgh a bheireadh iad às na thuirt e.

'S e bha thall 's a chunnaic, gun teagamh. A' dol dhan iomain 's
dhan a' bhall-choise 's do thòrraidhean air feadh na dùthcha. 'S
gu eilthireachdan nas fhaid' air falbh. Gu bainnsean nuair a
gheibheadh e cuireadh, rud nach fhaigheadh ach uair ainneamh.
Cha chuireadh e dragh sam bith air am beul-bòidheach a thoirt
do na mnathan eadar seo 's Am Parbh. Chluinneadh a h-uile tè
dhiubh na bha i 'g iarraidh cluinntinn. Nach do ghabh e splaoid
còmhla ri caileach-dhubh a bh' air a bhith thall thairis is ris an
do thachair e às dèidh aifreann ann an Cille Bhrìghde? Bha mar a
bhiodh e 'n ceann a chosnaidh rud beag na dhìomhair. Bhiodh e

a' càradh rothar is radios air chùl an t-seanchais agus televisions nuair nach robh ann ach an fheadhainn dhubh is gheal. Dh' fhaodadh e innse dhut anns an spot dè bha ceàrr air na gears no air an fhuaim no air an dealbh; co-dhiubh a ghabhadh a chàradh gus nach robh feum sam bith ann.

Ach mar bu trice b' ann ri meabadaich a bhiodh e ris. Seadh 's bha e pòsda cuideachd. Tè bheag bhìodach a thàinig à Geàrrloch a dh' obair air mhuinntearas anns an Taigh-Mhòr. A' Bheannag Bheannaicht' a bheireadh iad oirre gun fhiosda dhì fhèin. 'S i chumadh smachd air nan cumadh duine sam bith. Ach 's ann ainneamh ainneamh a chanadh i dùrd ann am fianais dhaoine, a-mach air a cuid ùrnaighean 's laoidhean.

'S ann aig Nì Math fhèin a bha fios ciamar a chaidh dhaibh aig an taigh. No fo na plaidichean. Rachadh aic' air an tosd marbh-tach ud a ghabhail oirre fhèin nan robh i den bheachd 's gun robh feum aic' air. Thachair iad nuair a choisich i fhìn seachad air fhèin oidhche da na h-oidhcheannan thall air Bealach an Duine Mhairbh. Thug i 'n t-sùil ud dha. No co-dhiù 's e sin a thuirt e mas fhìor nuair a bha 'n deoch air ri fear a chuir comhairle ris ciamar a gheibheadh e bean.

Gun teagamh, cha b' urrainn dhut fhulang ach fad ùine. Mu dheireadh thall fhuair e cùl na còmhla mach às a h-uile taigh-seinnse 's bookie sa bhaile mar thoradh air a' chabadaich 's obair-nan-dòrn, a dh' fhaodadh èirigh ann am prioba-nan-sùl. Fiù 's gus an là-'n-diugh chan urrainn dhut ainmeachadh air ainm ann an claisneachd cuid a dhaoine ged 's e balgairean 's bugairean a th' annta fhèin. Ma bheir thu tarraing air, thig cobhar-nan-con-cuthaich ri am beul. Iomairt chàirtean 's math dh' fhaoidte a thàinig gu crìch na blàr. No nuair a bha fios aca glan gun robh e dèanamh tàir mhòr orra ged nach dèanadh e ach sùil a chaogadh is 'Seadh?' a chantail ann an dòigh àraid.

Tha e na shìneadh anns a' Chlachan a-nis o chionn deich bliadhna gun bhìog aige ach na th' ann de sheanchas fhathast mu dheidhinn 's mu na thuirt e! Cha mhòr nach eil e ann fhathast, chanadh tu.

# Dawn Dweud

*Version in Welsh by Menna Elfyn, Ceredigion*

Yn ei ffordd droellog ei hun, roedd ganddo'r ddawn dweud, dim gair o gelwydd. O'r eiliad y cafodd ei ben bach ei fedyddio alle fe wneud pen a chynffon o bob copa gwalltog, a rhai o bob lliw a llun a lluniaeth.

A doedd yna neb nad oedd yn ei ddeall. Pobl o Gwmsgwt, Y Tymbl, Pentrecagal a Plwmp, o Gilfachreda, Tredomen, Abergwyngregyn, Llandisilio, Nebo a Rachub a Senghennydd. Dieithriaid pur a hocwyr da o du hwnt i Dre'r Clawdd, Gelli Gandryll, Y Fenni, Croesoswallt, yr Amwythig, Bryn Buga, Caerfaddon,Y Fan, Nanhyfer, neu Faesaleg. Alle fe wilia â nhw i gyd, a pho leia y dywedai, y mwya ystyrlon yr oedd e'n aml.

Wrth gwrs, roedd e'n deithiwr at ei wadnau. Angladdau, pererindodau, ledled y wlad. Ac ambell bererindod bellach bant. A phriodasau hefyd pan ofynnwyd iddo. A doedd hynny ddim yn fynych. Oedd e'n hen law ar siarad mwyn merched mwynach o fan hyn i Borthaethwy. Fe fydde pob un yn clywed y gan a'i swynai. Oni ddiflannodd unwaith gyda lleian o'r genhadaeth a ddaeth ar ei thraws ger Llyn Tegid? Roedd ei ffordd o fyw yn dipyn o ddirgelwch. Trwsio beiciau a phellebryddion diwifrau, er mwyn cael ceiniog ddistaw, a theledyddion hefyd yn nyddiau'r rhai du a gwyn. Alle fe reddfu beth oedd o'i le ar y gêrs neu ar y sain neu'r llun; os oedd gwellhad iddo neu beidio.

Ond yn fwy na dim, siarad oedd ei yrfa drwy'r byd. Ac oedd, roedd e'n briod. Pwten fach a hanai o Bentre Galar ac a fu'n howscipar unwaith i'r ffeirad. Swcwr Tragwyddol oedd ei llysenw, ymhell o'i chlyw wrth gwrs. Roedd hi'n gallu ei sgwaro fe os oedd rhywun yn gallu. Er doedd hi byth braidd yn agor ei cheg yn gyhoeddus ar wahan i ganu ar y galeri mewn cymanfa.

Sut oedden nhw'n tycio'n y tŷ, Duw a ŵyr. Neu'n rhannu'r cynfas. Roedd ganddi'n ei mynwes yr arf angeuol, tawelwch. Fe wnaethon nhw gwrdd pan gerddodd hi heibio iddo y tu allan i'r Llew Du ger mynwent Mathafarn. Neu dyna ei esgus e wrth iddo rannu'r gyfrinach gyda gŵr a geisiodd ei gyngor ar ddod o hyd i wraig.

Wrth gwrs, dim ond nawr ac yn y man y gallech chi ei ddioddef. Roedd e'n un a gafodd ei wahardd fesul un o bob tafarn a lle bwci yn y dre ar draul ei siarad bras neu'r hw ha a achosai am y nesa peth i ddim. Allwch chi ddim yngan ei enw o fewn milltir i ambell unigolyn; wic wews eu hunain gan fwyaf. Enwch e ac fe ddechreuan nhw wylltu a throi'n goch twrci. Gan efallai adrodd stori am gêmau cardiau a ddiweddodd mewn cnapan. Neu'r troeon y gwydden nhw eu bod yn destun ei ddigrifwch, hyd yn oed os mai codi ael yn unig a wnai gan wefuso 'Ym' mewn ffordd arbennig.

Deng mlynedd, ar orwedd, ym mynwent y llan heb na siw na miw allan ohono, y mae'r chwedlau'n dal yn fyw ac yn iach. Man a man a mwnci, ei fod o gwmpas heddi.

# PART FIVE

*Ah earth you old extinguisher.*
— Winnie: *Happy Days*

## The Weight of It

The years of chalk
and children's faces
never taught me to expect

that yesterday in sunshine
by open earth
I'd pray

perpetual light
might shine on one
that I saw grow

to give unbroken years
of nights and days
to a sick woman

until the lonely
weight of it
was told at last

on straining
rope from
a roof beam.

Last night this came
between me
and my sleep:

I ask forgiveness
of him if I ever
was unkind

when his was one
among the upturned
faces reading mine.

## In the Light of Dark

After he had set the tripod up
he ducked beneath the hood,
with lens aligned to catch
the harbour and the sky,
the breakwater with seagulls,
the tide just so, the boats
in correspondence,

the whole comprising all the light
that he intended to admit
in an unshuttered second
set to leave its mark upon
the plate's prepared emulsion.

With the tent about his ears
he does not foresee
the two small boys who
in that instant from stage left
appear upon the scene,

curious to know what's going on
beneath the hood, and never
dreaming they're already ghosts
on glass, already on their way
to meet us in a hundred years.

Now that we've arrived in time
to see the unintended boys
still wondering about the hooded man,
still waiting for something to be revealed,
we want to slip inside the frame and ask

*Who are you?*
*What became of you?*

We forget that if the boys could speak
they'd still be in the dark
about what will unfold for them
beyond the moment framed. So also
for the hooded man who let in light.

So also for ourselves,
looking on and in
with eyes that blink and peer
through the lens of now and here.

# Nights Out

*i.m. Tom the Bard Power, 1914-1999*

The times we could have had
over the years,
old friend,
but didn't.

Those nights we could have
stood or sat together
bending ears,
bending elbows,

smoking and talking
until closing time
or after

doing our health
no good at all,
but lacing our hearts
with laughter

and leaving our spirits
fortified and fit
as fiddles.

All those nights
we could have
gone to town

over and above
the many times
we did.

Oh yes, old friend,
there's always that —

the many times
we did.

## The Light Returning

She's still there,
you're saying to yourself —
a woman you'd almost forgotten

until you happen to see her today
at the gate of her council house
with ash on her forehead

lifting up her head
as if she scented possibility
or presence in the air

remarking to a neighbour
about the great stretch
coming in the evenings.

Cloud shifts above the salmon
on the town's clock tower.
Bleached light floods the terrace,
finds the woman's face,
then seems to radiate from her grey hair,
her glasses and pale skin.

You feel it in yourself, as though
she's shared it with you.

Then you move on, past
the years of nights and days
since the Sunday in July
someone on the bridge
six miles downriver

saw the boat
drifting in midstream
and crossways to the ebb,

the Jack Russell whining
and shaking herself dry.

*It would do you good*
*to see the stretch*
*coming in the evenings*
she's repeating in the distance,

the woman who had tried
to grasp the tidings
of a summer afternoon

by telling and retelling
a litany of circumstantial
bits and pieces —

the new pinny with the pale blue
forget-me-nots that she was wearing,
the clock that was a wedding present
ticking on the mantel,
the Sacred Heart lamp needing oil,
the voice of Mícheál Ó Hehir
from the wireless on the sideboard

then in the air outside
the sudden wailing
of the Town Hall siren
as though there was a house on fire

and how she was thinking
that it was like the banshee
as she reached for two plates
to cover and keep warm

their dinners of roast beef
and mashed potatoes, with gravy
for Tommy and dressed
cabbage for his father,

and how she had just slipped
the dinners back into the oven
when some shadow crossed her heart
and the knock came to the door.

# Three Notes of One Day

PRELUDE

A small bird's
first note
with the dawn

gives me courage
though the bird
knows none.


THE HURLER

Often he rose
above himself

as he rose
above the ground.

Today there's a guard of honour
to see him going under.


MOON LANDING

The crescent moon
is on her back tonight,
a golden goddess
coming down.

It looks like
she might slip
through the trees
at Kyledroughtaun

just miss the river
and sink into a meadow
in Ballinderry.

## The Man and the Dream

I mean the sleeping man
thrown back on the bed

face to the ceiling
and mouth wide open —

the quiet man
(answers to Paddy)

with one leg outstretched
and the other

(the shapely one
in the nylon stocking)

standing between
the wardrobe and washbasin.

Yes, that's the leg
I'm talking about

and that's the man
who wears it whenever

he's expecting a visitor,
such as last Christmas

when, as it happened,
he needn't have bothered.

Yes, I mean that grey man
this Thursday afternoon

dead to the world
in Room 14.

I hope he's having the best
dream of his life

and that it lasts
forever.

## Lucy Sleeping by Firelight

Beyond the cottage window
November seeps up darkly
from the fields beside the sea
and meets itself descending
from Reilig a' tSlé' and Seana-Phobal,
from Suí Finn in the Monavullaghs
and Cruachán in the Comeraghs.

Tonight an open fire is all
our warmth and way of seeing,
with ash and ember whisper
and leap of light and shade
from hearthstone to dark
rafters overhead.

You're snug and sleeping
in my arms when suddenly
in turning shadow you become

more than a dreaming child,
my familiar flesh and blood
whose little name means light —

suddenly across your face
as out of immemorial mist

an image
of all the mothers
you carry within you.

## Thirteen Souls with Bread and Wine

The blind man
behind the pillar.

The bent woman
on two sticks.

The man with two pens
and a stone
in his pocket.

The bad singer
who always sings.

The dancer
who may have to have
her breast removed.

The priest whose mind
is elsewhere.

The mother who always brings
a Christmas dinner
to the cemetery.

The man who hooked
and lost the only
salmon of his life.

The nun who is beginning
to forget the days.

The man who plays
bass drum in the band.

The woman who paints
her toenails red
in summer.

The sergeant who overcame
the demon.

The baker's wife
lighting one candle
from another.

# PART SIX

## *Textament*

*The wise man is astonished by everything.*
— André Gide

# DOMAINS IN FLUX: *charting context and subtext of 'The Carrick Nine'.*

The only manuscript copy of 'The Carrick Nine' known to exist was anonymously deposited at Carrick-on-Suir Heritage Centre in the autumn of 2002, reputedly after it had been salvaged from a rubbish skip and had passed through several hands at various locations within the town. Though the pages were stained and somewhat tattered, material restoration and consolidation proved possible, along with a necessary degree of textual decipherment.[1]

Composed in a robustly traditional style, the ballad chronicles an outing by a party of local men, allegedly inebriated, who sailed downriver from Carrick to Waterford on June 12, 2001. An incident at Waterford resulted in their pursuit upriver by the police. The latter summoned the assistance of reinforcements who approached downriver, thereby ensuring a pincer-like interception of the fugitives. The men (locally labelled 'The Carrick Nine') subsequently appeared in court, charged variously with the larceny of kegs of beer, drunkenness, and obstructing Gardaí in the performance of their duties.[2]

Although the term is adopted hereunder for convenience, it is misleading to speak of an authoritative 'text' in relation to a composition which is essentially oral in character and hence open to modification in the course of transmission or performance. The 'text' in this case to some extent remains fluid; it may be altered or amended deliberately and consciously, or inadvertently through faulty recollection or even confusion due to a lack of sobriety on the part of the singer or reciter on particular occasions. It can of course be argued that all versions are equally 'valid' as socio-verbal constructs and cultural signifiers.[3]

---

[1] The Carrick-on-Suir Heritage Centre received advice and assistance from the National Library of Ireland, the Royal Irish Academy (Institute for Advanced Studies), the Linen Hall Library (Belfast) and the British Library (British Museum).

[2] See *The Munster Express*, Waterford, 1 February 2002, banner headlined **'Four Hour Chase as Nine Carrick Men Launch Boat Raid on Waterford City: river drama as dramatic scenes unfold'**.

[3] See Umberto Eco's *A Theory of Semiotics* (1976) and *Semiotics and the Philosophy of Language* (1984) and especially his paper *L'opera in movimento e la coscienza dell' epoca* ('The poetics of the open work').

Even before the emergence of a manuscript text (with its musical notation), the ballad had reportedly already begun to acquire oral currency as a spoken 'recitation', or as a song, or as a combination of both recitation and song in order to lend variety to the presentation of a rather lengthy lay of twenty stanzas. The deployment of such archaic social strategies of poetic 'performance' could be viewed as evidence of ancient bardic practice having left a vestigial footprint deep in the popular unconscious.

'The Carrick Nine' may be stylistically categorized within the context of 19th-century street ballads, a genre which was shaped during the period and process of rapid linguistic transition from the Irish to the English language. Gaelic models exert a strong influence, especially in syntactical inversion, noun-adjective precedence, assonance, alliteration and internal rhyming, and a typical fondness for Latinized words such as 'deleterious', 'nefarious' etc.

The metre employed in the ballad is a somewhat loose usage of the traditional *ochtfhoclach beag*, a commonly occurring one in Irish song. The immediate musical and metrical model is the rollicking drinking song '*Preab 'san Ól*' by the Mayo poet Riocard Bairéad (1739-1819), composer of a body of witty and satirical verse. 'Preab 'san ól' is the abbreviated form of an exhortatory phrase meaning 'keep the drink going around'. The *ochtfhoclach* metre was used by Bairéad's contemporary John Philpot Curran in 'Let us be merry before we go' ('The Deserter'). The latter is said to have been imitated by Byron in 'Could love for ever / Run like a river, / And Time's endeavour / Be tried in vain . . .' It was also successfully used by Swinburne in his 'Anima Anceps'. Other uses of the metre in Anglo-Irish balladry and verse tend towards a vein of parody and doggerel, as in 'The Groves of Blarney' by Richard A Milliken, and 'The Bells of Shandon' by 'Father Prout' (Francis Sylvester Mahony). The *ochtfhoclach* metre is not easy to use in an elegant or serious manner in English.

The intended '*Preab 'san Ól*' tune to which 'The Carrick Nine' may be sung is in triple or 3/4 time but somewhat slower than the waltz. The strong rhythmic pulse and accentuated style is much closer to the mazurka.[4]

The traditional unaccompanied singing style uses strong accentual stress, emphasized by sudden glottal stops and the marked use of nasalization. Occasionally the metre dictates transfer of syllabic stress within a word in a way that may run counter to normal spoken usage.

Every text carries sociological subtexts embedded within it and 'The Carrick Nine' is no exception. Some revealing aspects of the socio-cultural assumptions of the society that produced both the actual escapade and its ballad narrative are significantly reflected in the mono-ethnic and mono-gender makeup of the participants. Unreconstructed patriarchal stereotype requires the 'wives and lovers' to remain at home while the symbolic hunter-gatherers set off on their exploratory excursion. While not made explicit in the ballad, it is also probably safe to ascribe an exclusively heterosexual orientation to the Nine, notwithstanding the text's pervasive implication of close male bonding and solidarity within the group.[5]

This brings us to the unresolved question of the ballad's authorship. By definition, since it narrates an event which occurred in June, 2001, its composition is recent, however antique the stylistic template. Yet the authorship of the work (inscribed 'Anon' in the manuscript) remains unknown. Locally the author is invariably assumed to be male, an assumption which is in itself revealing. An investigation seeking to identify the manuscript's handwriting would not be feasible and neither can it automatically be assumed that the author and the scribe (who possessed a competent degree of musical literacy) are one and the same.

Field research involving interviews with local people produced a uniform response, but no actual information. A stock reaction amounting to enigmatic verbal formula was very often encoun-

---

4 Originating in 16th-century Poland, the mazurka spread throughout Europe during the 18th and 19th centuries, and in art music was made famous by Chopin's approximately 60 works in the genre. Rhythmically somewhat similar in the Irish traditional music context is the Varsovienne, sometimes known colloquially in Co Clare, with erroneous etymology, as the 'Verse of Vienna'. 'Mazurka' became mazolka in Monaghan, mazorka in Donegal, myserks in Clare and mesorts in Kerry.

5 It is only in recent years that Irish society began to move towards equal opportunities legislation and some discussion of positive discrimination or mandatory quotas in relation to disadvantaged groups or minorities.

tered. In response to the question 'Who do you think wrote 'The Carrick Nine'?', the recurring reply almost invariably tended to be 'Sure you know yourself . . .'[6]

It has been suggested that this phrase is a typical example of inquisitional deflection and verbal evasiveness inherent in the post-colonial psyche. Such a glib analysis is in itself evasive, not to say superficial. There may be more behind the phrase 'Sure you know yourself' than contemporary critical discourse commonly allows for in its standard deconstruction of Irish vernacular codes. In fact it may not be entirely fanciful in this instance to suggest a hidden local impress of thought and culture which could be Hellenic in origin — in particular the striking resemblance between the phrase and the proverbial injunction 'Know Thyself' (*Γνῶθι σαυτόν*) inscribed on the temple of Apollo at Delphi and ascribed variously to Socrates, or by Plato to the Seven Wise Men.

While it may not be possible to prove or disprove conclusively such an apparently improbable cultural congruence, there is some local historical context worthy of consideration. Carrick-on-Suir was at its cultural, social, demographic and economic zenith from the mid to the late 18th century, with a population amounting to double the current figure of 5,000-odd. One of its most renowned residents was the polymath Patrick Lynch (1754-1818), scribe, schoolmaster and author and a classical and Gaelic scholar with a national reputation. Lynch directed his own Classical Academy and also owned the Carrick theatre. Several of his works of scholarship were published and printed in the town, which was rather grandiloquently styled 'The Athens of Munster' in *Finn's Leinster Journal* of December 1783.[7] Lynch was part of the learnèd and convivial Carrick circle which habitually met at a Cider Lane inn called The Oracle Arms, where, according to a contemporary chronicler[8]:

---

[6] In this vernacular usage the stress invariably falls on the final syllable, i.e. 'your*self*'.

[7] Lynch's publications included *The Pentaglot Preceptor: or Elementary Institutes of the English, Latin, Greek, Hebrew and Irish Languages* (Carrick-on-Suir 1796).

[8] Séamus Anaithnid Mac Conmara, sometime diarist and scribe, in a 1779 addendum to a Gaelic manuscript (Oxf Bod e 3/31531).

'the liveliest Wits of the town frequently muster to dine upon Beefsteak and French wine and Brandy, while engaging in repartee, Scholarly debate, Gossip and Conundrum through the medium of the Irish, English, Greek and Latin tongues. The overseer of all such Platonic Expostulation and Socratic Surmise is the genial landlord, Nioclás Mór Fear Feasa Mac Craith, nicknamed Oracle Magrath[9] in English . . .'

The durability of embedded tradition and historical accretion is a noted if not notorious characteristic of Irish culture. It may not be entirely fanciful to suggest that the enigmatic vernacular response 'Sure you know yourself' may still incorporate a faint echo of the Delphic injunction once well known in Carrick and perhaps still impressing its unrecognized ghost-presence upon folk culture.

If identification of the authorship of the ballad has so far drawn an investigative blank, something of the same frustration has surrounded attempts to elicit local information about the personalities and socio-economic profiles of some of the protagonists in the actual episode which was its catalyst. Some were said to be 'out of town at the moment'; others were said to be 'barred' from popular local hostelries. All proved to be unavailable for interview, with one reputed to be in Limerick prison.

There are diverse perceptual and existential domains overlapping here, of which the mode of anonymity is one. Some scholars of language theory and communication process have come to posit the re-emergence of a predominantly oral culture based upon the immediacy and ubiquitous availability of mass-media technology. In a one-dimensional and present-continuous flow of now 'the past' does not exist. Similarly, as in all oral cultures, a single identifiable authorship of a 'text' is not seen as significant; the verbal 'story' simply subsists as common property within the flow, unanchored to any singular editorial or authorial identity. The present writer has accordingly concluded that this exegesis of 'The Carrick Nine' should share concordance with its sub-

---

[9] A much weathered and partially fragmented gravestone at the medieval St Nicholas burial ground off Main Street carries the name Magrath and what appears to be some Greek lettering. The memorial may mark the grave of the one-time landlord of The Oracle Arms.

ject's communality by a similar authorial immersion within the unbiddable flux of oceanic anonymity.[10]

It finally remains to consider briefly the archetypal and generic 'ports of call' relevant to narrative patterns discernible or inferred in 'The Carrick Nine'. The range, considered both spatially and temporally, is quite considerable. The textual reference to *An Slua Muirí* (the Gaelic name for the Irish naval reserve, loosely meaning 'the sea-host') implies mythic reference beyond the river and into the global continuum. The range of symbolic quest even goes boldly beyond the terrestrial domain. In the final stanza there is an oblique textual reference to the cult science-fiction television series *Star Trek* and its galactic outreach.

Some historically remote genre-links with the ancient literature of Ireland may be tentatively posited — with, for instance, the *Echtra* or 'adventure journey' tales, most often telling of the journeys of human beings towards an idyllic otherworld. Closely allied to the *Echtra* are the *Immrama* or 'Voyages'. The earliest of these is the essentially pagan eighth-century *Immram Brain* or 'Voyage of Bran', while a late ninth-century Christian and Latinized example is *Navigatio Brendani*.[11]

Much closer in time as a popular literary model is a self-parodying riverine genre of mock-heroic nautical adventure and mishap.[12] The existential freedom of the river also has obvious thematic parallels in Mark Twain's *The Adventures of Huckleberry Finn*, while textual reference to piracy playfully invokes the genre of swash-buckling and romantic Errol Flynn movies such as *Captain Blood* (1935)[13], popular between the nineteen thirties and fifties in 'the picture house' of every small

---

[10] Copies of the paper are to be assigned in anonymous format to the standard repositories; other copies will be released into the stream of happenstance by being discreetly 'dropped off' at randomly chosen public locations. The strategy is meant to promote fortuitous encounter, in concordance with the 'message in a bottle' mode.

[11] See Murphy, Gerard, *Saga and Myth in Ancient Ireland*, Mercier Press, Cork 1971.

[12] For a River Suir-based example of the genre see 'The Wreck of the Gwendoline' by CJ Boland, *My Clonmel Scrapbook*, E. Downey, Waterford 1907. Other examples include 'The Wreck of the Mary Jane', *Irish Street Ballads*, ed. Colm O Lochlainn, The Three Candles, Dublin 1939.

[13] Co-starring Olivia De Havilland.

Irish town and hence formative elements of the communal imagination and its folkloric templates of the heroic, especially in communities with some sailing and fishing tradition.[14]

In fact there was some history of piracy on the river Suir, and it was specifically linked to Carrick Beg, the south-bank suburb of Carrick-on-Suir. In March 1734 a number of Waterford merchants felt obliged to petition Lionel, Duke of Dorset and Lord Lieutenant of Ireland, to take steps for the suppression of piracy on the river. They complained that cargoes of grain, beer and other goods originating in Clonmel and proceeding downriver towards Waterford were being seized en route by the 'common people' at Carrick Beg, who were grown 'so Tumultuous' that no craft could enjoy safe passage. His Excellency was implored to take steps to ensure that 'the Rioters were suppressed, Liberty given to bring down goods, and the Navigation more Free . . .'[15]

Below Carrick-on-Suir the tidal river is dramatically transformed from pastoral to estuarial, anticipating its own imminent transfiguration and consummation — along with its sister rivers Nore and Barrow — within the cosmic continuum of 'salt, estranging sea' beyond Waterford Harbour.[16] The mature waterway on which these questing pilgrims sail towards the estuary not only constitutes the boundary between counties Kilkenny and Waterford, but also between the provinces of Leinster and Munster and the ancient tribal territories of Ossory (*Osraighe*) and Decies (*Déise*). Atavistic tribal antagonisms embedded in ancestral loci of place and communal memory express themselves ritualistically and symbolically in modern times through hurling, an ancient field game of great speed and skill in which shapely wooden bats known as hurleys, hurls or *camáin* are wielded by opposing teams on stirring public occasions of assembly and contention.

While there is no immediately overt Homeric parallel evident

---

[14] The weather-vane over Carrick's landmark 18th-century Town Clock at the West Gate of the town takes the significant form of a salmon. See Coady, Michael, *Oven Lane* (1987/2001) and *All Souls* (1997/2001), The Gallery Press.

[15] p.306, *The Story of Waterford*, Edmund Downey, Waterford 1914.

[16] Like its sister rivers Nore and Barrow, the river Suir (*An tSiúir*, i.e. the sister) is mentioned by Spenser: 'The first the gentle Shure, that, making way / By sweet Clonmel, adorns rich Waterford'; Book iv, canto xi, *The Faerie Queen*.

in the Carrick Nine text, it should perhaps be borne in mind that the actual excursion occurred within the octave of Bloomsday, and that the potency of primal archetype subsists in its timeless subterranean universality at the level of the unconscious.

The waterway of the lower Suir signifies a kind of no-man's 'land' where territorial and tribal imperatives are in flux and the layered social organization of land-based settlement is in conditional abeyance. If the boat's habitual Carrick berth represented a secure *omphalos*[17], it follows that as the Nine sail downriver they are voyaging beyond the safe sanctuary (Gaelic *tearmann*) of Tipperary South Riding and entering the hazardous confluence of 'cross-currents where three counties meet', with the Scylla and Charybdis of Leinster-Kilkenny to port and Munster-Waterford to starboard.[18]

Singing a love song to Nancy Spain as they go, the free-spirited Carrick Argonauts consume a Circaean beverage in the form of 'copious draughts of cider'. Already afloat on their native river, the Nine have also entered a fluid interior world within which the boundaries of perception tidally wax and wane as they sail on. This motif of Dionysian buoyancy is carried further: when they reach the quayside of Waterford — with its *urbs intacta* motto suggesting an inviolate integrity — they are there tempted not by flesh and blood Sirens, but by barrels of Smithwick's beer, one of which they succeed in carrying off. As they attempt to seize another they are suddenly confronted by the guardians of the citadel, alerted to their invasive arrival by a Cyclopean surveillance camera.

In the ensuing river-chase their mistaken identification as major criminal suspects brings down upon them a veritable fleet of land-based avengers. The hubris and exhilaration with which

---

[17] i.e. world navel and centre. Located on the slopes of Mount Parnassus, the Oracle of Delphi stood at the crossroads of the ancient world. Zeus, the chief Olympian god, released two eagles. One he released from the East (the Ascendant), the other he released from the West (the Descendant). At the point where the two eagles met, Zeus then threw a Sacred Stone marking the *omphalos* or navel of the world at Delphi.

[18] Though formally, legally and administratively located in the extreme southeast corner of Co Tipperary, Carrick-on-Suir is actually ambiguously perched on the river boundary with Co Waterford and only a mile from the Kilkenny/Leinster border which is also defined by a river, the Lingaun, a downstream tributary of the Suir. The boundaries are literally fluid.

they set out on their voyage has attracted the envy and anger of the Fates. The Nine are accordingly enmeshed in inexorable and humiliating entrapment. They are literally brought back to earth. Even before their court appearance and subjection to the public retribution of legal process, they must first undergo a more intimate interrogation and trial as, 'sick, sore and sorry', they make their crestfallen way home 'to face their wives'. In one form or another it seems that the Sirens are inescapable.

All ends well, however, since the day's adventure has fortunately involved no loss of life. Let off lightly by the judge in court — who reserves his main criticism for the ludicrous over-reaction of the forces of law and order — the Nine emerge as folk heroes who receive national media attention. The ballad not only extols their 'dash and daring' — while diplomatically including a good word for the police — but also enjoins posterity to ensure the continuance of their 'name and fame' through the deliberate communal adoption, possession and performance of the text which it provides for that very purpose.

Thus the text self-referentially invents and fuels the engine of immortality for its own narrative, since it not only enters into and anchors itself within communal keeping but in so doing also energises the very consciousness it penetrates, as a boat asserts dynamic form in the water it displaces while under way, creating the bow waves and stern wake that constitute its existential manifestation of exteriorized temporality. The 'waterness' of the water, as it were, cosmologically defines, releases and reveals the 'boatness' of the boat, and vice versa: in Joycean terms, each epiphanizes the other. This interpenetrative and fecund coupling of text with the reality that it both synchronically denotes and diachronically connotes succeeds in simultaneously exploiting and subverting some basic semiotic assumptions of post-modernist theory by circumnavigating the fluid parameters of its consensually adduced perceptual paradigms.

One can only surmise about how the composition might have been received by Nioclás Mór Fear Feasa Mac Craith and his learnèd clientele at The Oracle Arms in Cider Lane . . .

# The Carrick Nine

Air: *Preab 'san Ól*

### 1

One pleasant morning in this new millennium
    The summer sun was beaming down,
As a hardy skipper and his companions
    Cast off and sailed out from Carrick town.
They embarked with no premeditation
    Or contemplation of piracy,
They were well-provisioned against dehydration,
    With no inclination to mutiny.

### 2

The tide was full and their craft was shipshape
    And decked out bravely in blue and white,
They little thought as they turned downriver
    That this June day wouldn't turn out right.
While other men were slaves to duty
    And tied down to production-lines,
They had the freedom of the river
    This Monday morning of their lives.

### 3

'Farewell,' they cried, 'to Carrick Castle,
    The hill, the bridges and the town,
And *au revoir* to our wives and lovers,
    Expect us after the sun goes down.
The day is opening out before us,
    Who knows what's waiting around the bend?
The sky is blue and the birds are singing,
    Long enough we'll all be dead!'

### 4

The lower Suir is a noble river,
   Broad and deep in each bend and reach.
They'd a skipper skilled in navigating
   Cross-currents where three counties meet.
They struck up shanties like 'Carrickfergus',
   'A Hard Day's Night' and 'Nancy Spain',
Helped on by copious draughts of cider
   That served to keep their spirits raised.

### 5

By Fiddown Bridge they were in fine fettle
   And there decided to sail on,
They throttled up for their destination —
   The Déise city of Waterford.
The Latin motto of that metropolis
   Means the city that was never sacked —
The Carrick Nine were set to challenge
   Its reputation as *urbs intact*'.

### 6

On they went by Rockett's Castle
   Then swung north in the Long Reach
Where they say a Viking longship
   Lies buried fifteen fathoms deep;
Past Grannagh Castle sacked by Cromwell
   Then east by the rock of Bilberry
Until standing high on the horizon
   Were Gracedieu and Mount Misery.

## 7

When they reached the city all hands were famished
  With liquid rations almost drained,
Then their lookout spied upon the quayside
  A large consignment of kegs of ale.
The Nine were not men prone to plunder,
  They were no bloodthirsty privateers,
But that apparition was a fierce temptation
  To mortal men with a lust for beer.

## 8

They'd a keg on board and another hoisted
  When suddenly all hell broke loose;
That yard was under intense surveillance
  And a Garda squad car sped into view.
'Cast off me hearties!' the skipper shouted,
  'We'll quench our thirst on Tinhalla Quay,
Where our forefathers often landed salmon
  And brewed up gallons of strong black tea!'

## 9

The Carrick Nine ploughed off upriver
  Thinking that they were safe afloat,
But the men in blue were out to get them —
  They straight-away commandeered a boat.
So here beginning was a chase most thrilling
  That would continue for several hours,
This naval tussle would test the muscle
  And sailing skills of the civil powers.

## 10

The pursuing Gardaí grew alarmed as
    The Carrick craft seemed to pull ahead;
They radioed for reinforcements
    And declared a high security alert.
They suspected big-time operators
    Dealing in cargoes of contraband —
These fleeing raiders must be captured
    And brought to justice upon the land.


## 11

The Harbour Board was soon alerted
    And the South-East Fishery patrol,
An Slua Muirí and a helicopter
    Went on standby in Waterford.
Police were summoned from around the region
    With urgent orders to waste no time;
Twenty lawmen came swiftly speeding
    To meet the threat of the Carrick Nine.


## 12

The wildlife never knew such action
    In the calm expanse of that waterway;
Swans and salmon were in a panic
    And trout were traumatized that day.
Boats came racing and making waves as
    Angry expletives were employed —
Words deleterious and names nefarious
    Flew fast and furious across the tide.

### 13

As the chase proceeded it became apparent
    There was no escape for the Carrick craft,
For it was trapped in a pincer movement
    With the Law advancing both fore and aft.
Boathooks were brandished at close quarters
    There were some dangerous attempts to ram,
One Garda tumbled into the river
    But happily came to no harm.

### 14

Pollrone's the place where the nine were captured
    It'll be remembered forevermore;
Statements were taken and charges drafted —
    This escapade would end up in court.
The Carrick Nine made their way homeward,
    Sick, sore and sorry to face their wives;
Their trip had ended in disaster
    But luckily with no loss of lives.

### 15

When it came to court the lawyers wrangled
    About jurisdiction and piracy,
The saline content of river water
    And whether 'High Seas' embraced estuary.
Statutes were dusted dating back to
    The Great Armada and Francis Drake,
But the accused men pleaded the affair was simply
    A harmless spree and a big mistake.

## 16

In his summing up the judge was scathing
    About the waste of Garda time
And all the manpower that had been mustered
    To apprehend the Carrick Nine.
He imposed fines and applied probation,
    The sentences were rather light,
Since the only losses were a keg of Smithwick's
    And a sergeant's cap that sank out of sight.


## 17

Outside the court there was pandemonium
    And loud commotion as the men walked free.
The media went into feeding frenzy
    With microphones and photography.
There were mobiles trilling and reporters milling
    To grab some in-depth interviews;
This had the makings of a movie
    Or a Prime Time special after the News.


## 18

The names of all could be related
    But I'll just mention their captain, Ben,
He made the papers and raised the flag for
    A famous family of fishermen.
Carrick people know their boatmen
    Are not found wanting when there's need,
They've often come to people's rescue
    In times of river emergency.

## 19

Fair play also for those who're sworn
    To be our guardians of the peace,
None of us could walk in safety
    Without their presence on our streets.
So spare a thought for those policemen
    Who were not trained for naval tasks,
And ne'er before set foot on water
    To apprehend a pirate craft.


## 20

Now to conclude and close my story
    Concerning history and river lore,
God's blessing on our intrepid mariners
    Who boldly went where none did before.
Their dash and daring was quite amazing
    As delineated in these lines,
Sing on posterity to ensure longevity
    For the name and fame of the Carrick Nine.

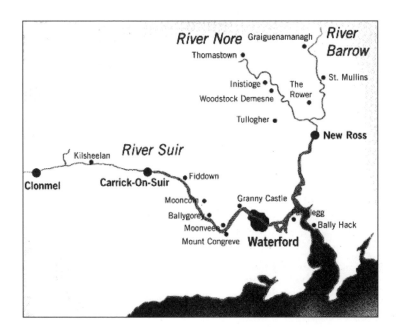

# PART SEVEN

*New Year's Eve*

*Early or late, all meet at the ferry.*
— Arab saying

## On the Record

At the end of the old woman's song
hear warm hands clapping around her
in the Connemara kitchen

and across the wear of years
bystanders' voices praising with
*Nár laga Dia thú**

and a dog, excited,
yelping on the side.

The song the old woman sang
told of beauty and love
and a drowning.

She learned it when she was young
from the boat-builder's sister
who left for Chicago and never
was heard of after.

The day of her singing was caught
by a man from The Folklore Commission

recording the sound of salvation
and also of blind-eyed innocence

in the year of the Warsaw ghetto,
packed trains pulling into Treblinka.

*May God not weaken you.

# Twelve Warm Coats, 1802

*My kind and Constant friend Joe Hearn was buried. He left £500
to the poor and Twelve Warm Riding-coats to 12 men of the town
whom his Executors (myself and Richard Sause) would deem most in
need.*

  — Ms journal, 1787-1809, of James Ryan, Carrick-on-Suir

> Who the chosen twelve were
> we will never know
>
> nor whether some sold off the gift
> for want of food or drink
>
> or whether all stayed clad
> against the cold and rain
>
> until the coats outwore them
> to serve others in their turn
>
> down to famished tatters
> on fetid straw.
>
> No shred of this remains, with
> kind and constant friends
>
> and twelve men warmly
> clothèd from the grave
>
> and every stitch and seam
> of every coat, and all
>
> poor flesh they sheltered
> long since dust. All gone,
>
> all gone — but for quill
> and candlelight, a warm

hand telling of a kindness
done, reaching

beyond clay to touch
this hand in turn.

## Sleeping Together

*It was the time when first sleep begins for weary mortals and by the gift of the gods creeps over them most welcomely.*
                                                              — Virgil

Her pillowed head by his,
they sink again in sleep
and through the night's

deep reaches
neither hears
the Town Clock bell

upon each hour,
the sough of wind outside,
the creak of branches —

she in a dream
of choosing shoes and dresses
with her sisters,

he breathing heavily
as he crosses in a boat
a flooded river.

He turns and lifts
an outstretched arm to fix
a mooring-rope across her;

unconsciously she twists
towards him and he turns
the other way.

Snug against his back
she's talking about colours
with her sister Margaret

who suddenly becomes
a stranger at a doorway
in another country;

beside her he's
unloading fish
with his dead father

while the flood has disappeared
around a bend to leave
a dried-up river.

Apart and intimate
they venture on
and never meet until grey

morning with the swish
of rain insinuates itself
across their eyelids.

As they reach the same horizon
and begin to speak
the night's affairs already slip

downstream, to fade
into complicit light where
dreams lie down to sleep.

# Rain on the Cards

The man from Deerpark
claimed he could read the cards
and was convinced of a conspiracy
to rob us of the sun.

Most days he cycled into town
for bread and talk,
the obsession throbbing under the cap
and hungry for a hearing.

*Isn't it shockin'?*
*Isn't it shockin' to the world?*
*And there's worse on the way for tomorrow.*

What else he could see in the cards
he said he dared not tell
since people were better off
not knowing what was on the way:
soon enough they'd meet it.

Last night in a pub
I overheard his requiem:

*A harmless man,*
*but he'd drive you cracked*
*about the weather and the future.*
*And never out of the wellingtons,*
*the Lord have mercy on him.*

And so the word goes round
from mouth to mouth.
How he'd gone out
to check the cattle
before the storm

that he felt stirring
in his bones

and how his brother found him
face-down in the dark,
the wellingtons, the wet,

far beyond
all fields
or weather
or tomorrow.

## Orphans

On the third day
after my mother was buried
I went with my wife
to the bright honey-meadow
commonly called Clonmel.

In a junk shop
we didn't know was there
she picked up dirt cheap
a small dancing doll.

Isn't she lovely,
the woman exclaimed — wind
her up behind and round
and round she goes

until she slows.
I'm sorry I can't
keep her for myself
but I'm chock-a-block already.

At the back of the shop
I found a kitsch Madonna —
chipped frame, cracked glass,
reduced

(out of the house
next door, I'm told,
the one that's now
invisible).

People stare as we step
down the street
with these orphans
who've found a new home —

the doll to dance
on demand till whenever
the spring in her
gives up the ghost,

the cracked Madonna to lie
with Saint Joseph and the Sacred Heart
over our heads
in the space of sighs

where as you stoop under rafters
you might hear
the scrabble
of claws on roof tiles.

# Normal Singing

*The day is now well advanced. And yet it is perhaps a little soon for my song. To sing too soon is fatal, I always find. On the other hand it is possible to leave it too late. The bell goes for sleep and one has not sung.*
 — Winnie: *Happy Days*


The piano reclines in the bar's back room
where in all of its nights and days
it never knew caress
or climax of any kind of sonata.
It's missing two castors behind
and so leans back at its ease
in a corner where drinkers pass
to and fro with bladders full or relieved.

On the piano and around the room
are eleven pots of exotic flowers
that winter or summer never
need watering, and in the bar are seven
more pots of the same.

Over it all is Ellen, who has stood
by an open grave in her time
to see husband and son go down
and almost followed them there
on the wintry day she collapsed
in the yard and was out for the count
two hours on her own. Following which

she fought her way back and after six months
dusted off pots of flowers and threw
the front door open again
to people and drink and singing

for this is a house where lifetimes
of tipsy songs have been sung
and a place for the singsong still,
while the laid-back piano with flowers
just sits in the back room and listens.

It's taken for granted here
that every woman and man
must harbour some kind of a song

and if you should happen
to stumble or lose your way
then you'll be forgiven,
or helped along if anyone
else knows the words.

On New Year's Eve the bar is full
with spill-over into the room
of the waterless flowers
and laid-back piano, with songs
all around and tactful calls
now and then for a bit of hush.

Ellen's behind the bar, with Sheila
and Tommy and Margaret assisting,
and women done up to the nines for
the night that's in it. Colour it simple

and sacred, this mortal occasion
of souls assembled to mark
the flux between all that is gone,
and all the unknown to come.

Outside, a steady downpour
advancing from Slievenamon

courses over roof-ridges, slates
and gutters and windows and walls,
streaming down Lough Street, gurgling
into dark drains and off to the river,
then on and on to the sea forever.

As the old year runs out
the back door's unlocked to let it go.
Open the front then to flowing night
and face whatever may come.

Under the plenteous rain
that descends on the valley
midnight strikes on the Town Clock bell
that has measured the hours
for two hundred years

and there, slipping in from the dark,
the poet from Ayr just in time
with his presence as all join hands
and rise to his song together with
millions of others elsewhere
this night of old acquaintance.

Then round the house an exchange of well-wishing,
embraces and kisses and tears
before we return to replenishing glasses
and normal singing continues.

# How Goes the Night?

*for James*

A boy is playing
on the green

while autumn dusk
is coming down;

soon he will be
gathered in

to drink his milk
and brush his teeth,

hear a story
I will read,

then say his prayers
and go to sleep.

Why should this make me
want to weep?

*The face of time in the convent garden*

# The Star

*. . . there is no Now or Then for the Holy Ghost.*

— John Keats

Half of life is about just showing up, said Woody Allen. As if that was easy. On the way don't look straight on for revelation, since it's mostly dressed in the mundane, if there at all. Always a sideways glimpse in place and time, dimly discerned in the half-light and the maze of mutability.

So, if you're asking, it's only the regular practice of the parish choir. No more, no less, and barely hanging on against the odds. It calls for putting aside whatever you'd otherwise be doing any Thursday night, irrespective of the weather.

And place? Since all creation needs particular space to happen in? Though both space and time confound us, we live within their mystery. Reaching for metaphor. Living as if. As if our uncertain hopefulness might in itself shed light on one another. As if we know why we cannot but sing against the dark.

So what is the particular where of this?

Locate the lower valley of the Suir, the town named for a rock, and there, the unremarkable reality of upper William Street.

Go by the parish church of St Nicholas, patron of seafarers, scholars, brewers, bakers, pawnbrokers, perfumers, brides and children. Turn in beside it to the car park that was the convent garden for two hundred years, then by the railed-in corner where nuns' unloved bodies have metamorphosed into fundamental seed-bed and serenity of earth.

Find the side-door beside vandalized and boarded windows, then climb the narrow stairs past fallen plaster to the convent chapel, still intact in carved wood and marble and stained glass, with *Gloria in Excelsis Deo* and *Sanctus Sanctus Sanctus* lettered in rich gothic on sanctuary ceiling.

Over and around it all, the astounding possibility of soul.

Enter this abandoned sacred space, this place of showing up and showing forth, of gathered absence and presence. This place of silenced prayer and poor forked creatures. The craftsmen who carved and painted. You yourself, with those who've come to sing. Further back, veiled women in their generations shuffling

into place before first light to chant *Ave Maris Stella*\* while —
beyond the walls, within the walls — the attrition of the day
began and still begins.

In this lit upper room of the decaying building song sheets are
handed out and parts allotted to prepare the music of the season:
of Holy Week or Pentecost or Christmas and of all the ordinary
Sundays in between. From week to week the routine showing
up, the falling off, the loss and gain, the undervalued keel of
habit, courage, hope, humility.

Imperfection is the constant here, with men and women learn-
ing in uncertainty to sing. Join in if you wish, or else remain
aside, downstairs in the gloom, and hear the voices, less than
twenty, faltering above.

> *They lookèd up and saw a star*
> *Shining in the East, beyond them far;*
> *And to the earth it gave great light,*
> *And so it continued both day and night.*

\*Hail Star of the Ocean

134

# PART EIGHT

*The Beech in Winter*

*Tell me what am I.*
*First I'm five, second seven.*
*Third I'm five again.*

## 1

Boy on the roadside
weeping for his mangled dog.
Old grief of the world.

## 2

Time of two faces
bringing all things down to earth.
Snowdrops over ground.

## 3

Ashen on my brow,
a thumbprint map of Ireland.
Lenten streams are clear.

## 4

April dandelions
take each verge and open space
in their spring campaign.

## 5

Inside my old school
a wayward scent in ambush.
I'm back in a desk.

## 6

Jackdaw perched on high
dumps on my new overcoat.
She says it's a sign.

## 7

First Communion day.
Two faces in that picture
commune from the dark.

## 8

The stoup in the porch
holds two hundred years of hands
and holy water.

## 9

Rooks are tuning up
for *Le Sacre du Printemps*.
Ageless *avant-garde*.

## 10

My mother's fiddle
has been moved to the top shelf.
The higher silence.

## 11

The hill's easier
if you follow the faint track
of the Famine road.

## 12

When that mouth opens
be sure to keep your distance.
It swallowed two farms.

## 13

Thirty feet beneath
Pat's Fast Food and Takeaway,
Ice Age river-bed.

## 14

Grey of winter sea
makes her long for warm embrace,
stormy nights in bed.

## 15

*Oh Jesus tonight!*
Her hot love-cry as they hit
the final furlong.

## 16

Mahler's daughter died
post-*Kindertotenlieder*.
His wife's fear confirmed.

## 17

Driving to the West
I turn up the stereo:
deaf Beethoven's *Ninth*.

## 18

And who else *woz 'ere*?
The full of the town, no less,
over and over.

## 19

Struggle in small hours
to undo the tangled lace
I tied this morning.

## 20

My son is obsessed
with skateboard glide and take-off.
The Icarus thing.

## 21

During the Mozart
she scribbles on the programme:
*Pick up dry cleaning.*

## 22

When you're just thinking
you needn't wear your glasses
or have the light on.

## 23

While I was sleeping
the highest tide of the year
slipped in and slipped out.

## 24

The wind roared all night.
It pawed all doors and windows,
then slunk off at dawn.

## 25

Virgin reflected
upside down in Clareen Well.
Water boatmen dance.

## 26

He's alone tonight
but hopes the Muse might drop in,
now the coast is clear.


## 27

The beech in winter
flaunts its lovely nakedness
to seduce the spring.

# PART NINE

*Word of the Wind*

*Bob Dylan is givin' out Benediction up behind the chapel.*
　　　　　— Joe Flynn

# Whereabouts

Which or whether, think about all the feet of people walking around the town, men, women and children going and coming, coming and going, one direction or the other at the particular time that it happened to be, and whenever that was. Think about them all.

Maybe marching in bands or footing it in processions and funerals and fancy dress parades — drunk or sober, night and day, some in a hurry and some at their ease, shuffling along and going about their business. Up and down, over and back for years and years. Dogs and cats and horses and asses and jennets as well in their time and even an occasional elephant or camel out of Fossett's Circus, not to mention the fox that was going around every night last summer.

Imagine them all. Not just yesterday or last year or twenty years ago but for as long as the street was there, meandering along the same way as the river. When you add it all up which wore down which? Is it the feet wore the street or the other way around? And while you're at it how would you know whether someone was coming or going?

In any case the latest news is that they're digging up the Main Street today and dumping the bits of it into the bog — digging up the most important street around here since day one, whenever that was. They're breaking it up with picks and shovels, jackhammers and diggers and dumpers. They? Well you know yourself — the men doing the digging and the ones walking up and down talking on mobiles and the crowd in the Town Hall that are supposed to have the plan of everything.

It's a shocking kind of thing to see them digging up the street and hauling it away and dumping it into the bog beside the river, where it will never be seen nor heard of ever again. They say the surface is worn out and it must be replaced so that it can bear the traffic.

The most shocking thing of all is to stand there and see that under the street that they're breaking up there's nothing at all only ordinary dirt and the odd bit of an old drain. It might as well be anywhere. Or nowhere at all. Somehow I always thought that some part of all the things that ever happened here was hidden down there under the street. Like the bed of the river. But nothing at all, I tell you, only dirt. Ordinary dirt from anywhere, or clay if you like.

I'm not saying it matters at all but I'd like to pass on the history of this in case anyone ever comes along in the future and wants to know about the street and how it used to be and what happened to it. So I'm telling them that the broken bits of the street and every step ever made on it up to our time by man or beast, woman or child — the entire thing is being broken up in chunks and buried in the bog near the river, just up there beside the Clonmel road.

But hold on a minute. I just thought of something. This information about the whereabouts of the Main Street that was. It can only be right in years to come provided by then they won't be after digging up the bog itself, Main Street and all, and dumping it somewhere else. Because that would mean that you can't bank on any place anywhere staying put. For all we know, everywhere might have been somewhere else before it got to be where it seems to be now.

# The Waves

There was some money made on the mother's side of the family, for all the good it ever did anyone. Her father's sister Gertie had a great head for business. She could turn every penny into a shilling and every shilling into a pound. She bought the old boathouse at the end of the Prom in Tramore and made it a tea-house for day trippers out by train from Waterford.

You could get sliced ham there, and tea and bread and butter and sweet cake. Or even buy a kettle of boiling water to make your own pot of tea on the strand. She had a sign painted outside the old boathouse: GERTIE'S WATER IS ALWAYS ON THE BOIL.

She was a fine contralto and one of her great party-pieces was 'Alas Those Chimes' from *Maritana*. But she was disappointed in love and stayed bitter about men all her life. When she was twenty they say she fell head over heels for an insurance official from Cork. They were supposed to get engaged one Christmas. When she didn't hear from him she took the train down to Cork early in the new year and found her way to his address. His wife opened the door.

After that she concentrated on business and religion. And in the end most of the money she made went into stained glass windows and statues and chalices and marble side altars. Two things only you could be sure of, she used to say. The word of God and the waves of the sea.

It wasn't that she was over pious. She could swear like a trooper and deal with anyone. And she could put away whiskey, and sherry and port wine. Especially during Race Week in August. Playing cards with the horsey crowd in the Majestic until all hours, and delighted to take money off them.

But the religion went to her head in the end. When she was older she opened a huckster's shop. If the Angelus bell happened to strike while she was serving someone she'd suddenly stop and throw herself down on her knees behind the counter, giving out 'The Angel of the Lord declared unto Mary' and expecting the customer to respond with 'And she conceived by the Holy Ghost'.

One wild winter's night someone had to call the guards. Gertie was down on the Ladies' Slip in her nightdress. She was screeching into the storm, commanding the waves to be still.

# Pierced

Hello — Seventh Heaven? Is that Marie?

Of course I knew the voice right away. On one of the busiest days of the year. I thought she might only want to pick up the usual moisturiser, but no. Well, Sister, I said, it's Christmas Eve, and there's no way I could fit you in without an appointment. And as it is the power is going and coming all the time with the storm.

I didn't even bother telling her that slates were flying in all directions outside and, earlier on, the Carrick Brass Band had to run for cover into the hotel to play a few carols. Only ten minutes before, Liz was after dashing out the door and rescuing the retired PP of Fourmilewater, Father Gaule, when she spotted him losing his balance crossing the street and whirling around in the wind like the salmon on the Town Clock. The dazed old man was sitting in the salon surrounded by women under the dryers, waiting for a cup of tea and looking like he was just after landing on a strange planet.

But of course Perpetua never bothers with an appointment anyway. Because she was my teacher years ago she thinks she only has to waltz in and be seen to right away. It was the same only two weeks before when we had the Stand Up Sun Room launch. The place thronged, and in she breezes expecting immediate attention, pushing her way towards me and waving her voucher for the Slendertone special offer.

And this time, on a Christmas Eve in the middle of a hurricane, she was after deciding to get her ears pierced. After giving it careful consideration all week, mind you. Now Marie, she said, I know you won't refuse me, seeing as how it's the Lord's birthday tomorrow.

What in the name of Jesus has that to do with it? Of course I didn't say that. I still couldn't bring myself to take the Holy Name in vain in front of her and anyway how do you deal with someone well into her seventies and losing the run of herself since the Pope changed the rules and the Nuns' Wall was knocked? Do you know I'm a Bandon woman? she's always saying since they changed out of the long black habit. As if that was something special. The first time she came in to have her hair dyed she told me that she was twenty-five years below in the convent before she ever set foot in the Main Street, though it was only a hundred yards away.

Anyway I had to give in about doing her ears though God knows I'd enough on my plate already and the ham still waiting to be collected at Peggy Cooney's when we'd close up at five. So I managed to squeeze her in, and she was delighted with herself. And, in fairness, she gave me a decent Christmas tip, as well as leaving us a leaflet each on Some Practical Ways to Help the Holy Souls.

I always wanted to be pierced like my mother, she said. Before I go, I suppose a quick Turbo Bed session is out of the question?

# Blood and Ashes

My mother used to work one day a week cleaning the barracks at the time and she always said the constable was a harmless enough man that never done nothing to no one except going about his job. He was a Kerryman by the name of O'Leary. The most he ever had to do was arrest people for being drunk and disorderly.

They were troubled times of course. And it happened on a lovely evening in June when he was crossing the New Bridge with his dog, going for a walk around the hill of Carrick Beg like he did regularly. He had a golden retriever that everyone admired.

Two men came up out of the Bog Field, walked up to him and shot him dead. And then they disappeared up over the hill into the county Waterford. The news of what was after happening went around the town like wildfire. His body was brought on a cart down to the barracks and left for the time being on an old mattress on the floor of the holding cell until arrangements could be made and his people sent for.

Later on the Black and Tans arrived drunk from Clonmel and went on the rampage through the town, smashing shop windows in the Main Street and beating up anyone that would look crooked at them.

Everyone had an idea who the killers were but no one said anything. They couldn't have luck for what they done was what people thought in their own minds. Sooner or later they wouldn't have luck for it.

There was a lovely summer that year. The Truce was declared and the men on the run could show their faces again. Some were swaggering around and acting the cock of the walk, with guns on their hips and girls on their arms.

One of the constable's killers was called the Hillman. He was drinking one evening in a pub at the top of New Street. No one is sure exactly what happened. Some said a row over cards; others said it was over a woman. Others claimed it was an accident because of play-acting with guns. Anyway, whatever way it happened, the Hillman was shot dead.

And his body was brought on the same cart down to the barracks, and put on the same mattress in the cell. And his blood seeped through the mattress and down into ashes scattered on the floor under it, mixing with the blood of the man he killed.

My mother told me this. She was the one that had to clean the blood and ashes off the floor.

## Pal of My Cradle Days

I was only about five or six the first time I heard that song. Above at Town Wall there was a wedding party going on in Nancy Whittaker's. They're all dead now. And I was a little child living around the corner, excited, and running in and out of the wedding all day. Even the houses are gone now. The whole row that used to be there, including my uncle John's workshop with the piles of shavings and sides of coffins against the wall. Himself and his crooky pipe and hard hat and the plane in his hand. And his rhyme about the place.

> The Gorry Rue, that cursèd crew,
> The Long Lane and the Level too —
> The Town Wall at the head of them all!

No such thing as a closed front door in those days, except in wintry weather. And the crowd at the wedding *maith go leor*\* and giving me lemonade and sweet cake every time they noticed me under their feet. Whose child is that? they'd say. Don't drink that lemonade too fast now, or the gas will bring tears to your eyes and blow off your britches. Does your mother know where you are?

Someone was playing that song all day on a wind-up gramophone that was a wonder in them times. 'Pal of My Cradle Days'. Maybe they only had the one record. His Master's Voice. They kept putting that one song on all day.

I can hear it still.

\*tipsy enough

# The Five Useless Things

A mild spring day, with Billy Carty's love birds and budgies doing their nut in the aviary at the back of the house outside the cemetery. A big crowd, and a send-off you couldn't be too cut-up about, considering the man lived to near ninety. One of the Ryans from out in the county Waterford, near the holy well. No great tragedy, but respect is respect.

At the part where the priest sprinkles the grave with holy water and asks the Lord to send his angel to watch over it — that was when Tommy started shaking. Alongside my elbow, standing there between myself and Séamus. The two of us looked sideways at him. Head down, trying to hold it in. Answer me this, he muttered, out of the side of his mouth. I heard it from a woman in Cork. What are the five useless things in a man?

A fit of coughing. Mooney's truck groaning into gear on the road outside, turning up the hill to the piggery. Hardly a cloud in the sky all the way over the valley to Slievenamon. Lord have mercy, I responded to the priest along with the crowd. I'll tell you, said Tommy under his breath. The five useless things. As follows. Two tits with no milk. Two balls that can't hop. And a cock that can't crow.

Three of us choking together, chins down on our chests. Tommy between gasps explaining. From a woman I used to know in Roches Stores cafeteria. Near the Father Mathew statue. The priest to the rescue with a decade of the rosary, first glorious mystery, the resurrection, our father who art. All joining in bar one. And the budgies and love birds dancing sets of Lancers over the way.

# PART TEN

*The Place of Hurt and Healing*

*Foundlings near the fever hospital*

*And now good morrow to our waking souls,*
*Which watch not one another out of fear;*
*For love, all love of other sights controls,*
*And makes one little room an everywhere.*

— John Donne,
'The Good Morrow'

*In adults the heart is about five inches long and three and a half*
*inches across at its broadest point, and it weighs less than a pound.*
*An adult human being's heart beats on average about 38 million*
*times a year.*

## By Heart

Late in the evening
on the day I was opened
I resurfaced in intensive care,
high as a kite, or still half under,
hearing someone who turns out
to be myself babbling
texts I have by heart.

This castle hath a pleasant seat, I venture,
to an isle in the water with her would I go
and the little waves of Breffny
go stumbling through my soul.

You're grand, a Cork voice lilts,
bending to my ear through half-light hiss
and bleep. Your wife just slipped out
for a cup of tea. The job is done
with four bypasses, and your heart
is humming like the Kinsale roundabout.

What's your name? I ask.
Gemma, she said. Think of a jewel.
I will, I said or thought. Thou art more
lovely and more temperate.

Rest now, she said. I'll be here with you
all night. Good things of day begin
to droop and drowse, I try to say,
then drop off like a child to sleep.

## Extra-Corporeal Circulation

Where was I when my head was out of it?

Those hours on the table during which
with breastbone vertically severed
and ribcage opened wide

my heart and lungs were halted —
this heart that has been beating
beating, beating, beating, beating
since first pulse in the womb —

this most private core revealed,
lowered in temperature,
set at rest and ready for repair, with
my life's blood-flow sustained meanwhile
by *extra-corporeal circulation*
through the heart/lung machine
into which I'm plugged.

During this heart-arrested
interlude of several hours
in my one and only existence
although I was corporeally present and alive,

consciousness, unknown
to its own conscious self,
was provisionally elsewhere.

So where, for those hours, was this self-
scrutineer, this singular first person
that I alone
call I?
Myself.
*Mé féin.*

I visualize my open body lying there under the lights
the team around me in a place of healing,
bending to their learnèd art and craft, an art
as delicate and skilled and subtle
in its protocols as playing chamber music —

a group performance of artistry and grace,
of thinking and touching,
of speaking, signalling, responding,
of measuring, preparing, cutting,
swabbing, stitching, monitoring, mending.

Look in on it as might someone from another planet:
observe five robed members of the species *homo sapiens*,
most intimately tending to another of their kind
who lies utterly helpless under their hands.

These are sentient beings we call men and women,
here engaged in what is good and holy
but essentially akin to some others
of their species in the world, who
somewhere, anywhere, at this moment
surround another of their kind
to inflict appalling agony and terror
in prisons and interrogation chambers.

So be aware, you who might
look in on this from elsewhere:
the heart of *homo sapiens* has two faces
and the everyday reality
of human goodness is our constant
elevation and lifeline precisely because
it cohabits with the dark seed that always
waits its chance to germinate,
not just outside us but within.

Here I know I'm blessed
as I lie there in trust, open
and helpless, but in good hands.

Observe also how one part of the body
may be made to come
to the aid of another:

my inside left leg has been delicately slit
from ankle to thigh so that
saphenous vein may be *harvested*
(the leg can afford it)

and then recycled to make sections
of new plumbing intricately grafted
to carry living blood around
arterial roadblocks.

Flow is what it's all about.

And so this drama centred on my heart continued
through its set routines and rituals
while all around the everyday went on,
domestic sky shifting and remaking over Cork city,
its houses, streets and river, its traffic
and shopping centres, birds and trees,
its children coming home from school,
men and women at their work
or listening to music, reading, laughing,
walking dogs or calling on neighbours,
preparing meals or going to the bathroom,
talking or not talking to one another,
slipping toward despair or finding hope,
saying prayers and lighting candles
(some, I know, for me)

my wife meanwhile killing time
in the hospital, fretting between canteen
and waiting room and phone.

No one can throw light upon the mystery
of where was I throughout those hours —
where my memories and words and songs,
all the things I'd ever thought or felt,
the sum of all within my head and heart
that I call my self.

No surgeon can sort this Cartesian dilemma,
no anaesthetist,
no psychologist,
no scientist.

Months later I tried it
on a Clare musician
who's also a sculptor and shaper
and a freelance Buddhist.

Where was I,
I queried,
when I wasn't there?

Where else, he responded instantly,
only in the fourth dimension?
Wasn't I there once or twice myself?
It's a state of being, not a place,
and you can only know it
while you're in it.

That's telling me, I said.

# The Apple

Martin is almost free of pain today,
the tumour in his head still between
two minds about when to draw
the blinds for good.

Brigid sits by the bed,
methodically peeling
and dividing an apple,
handing him a slice.

What way is the budgie?
And the dog?
How's the garden, and all
the neighbours?

They're grand, she says.
They're grand.
And how is he
himself?

He bites on the apple.
I'm just waiting for the word
to tog out with the forwards
in the Munster Final.

Holy God Almighty Martin,
you're a gas man, so you are.
You were always a gas man.
Isn't that a lovely apple?

## Angels and Ministers of Grace

I dream that I am arguing in Irish
with the Pope and his *confrères*
about the ban on women priests.

*Mo náire thú, a Phápa,*
I lash out *go líofa,*
*tú féin agus seana-leaids an Chúria*
*ag swanáil timpeall is ag cogar mogar*
*in bhúr ngúnaí galánta corcra nó bána*
*faoi shíleáil iontach Mhícheálangelo.*[1]

Brazenly and fluently I make my case,
quoting to the holy fathers
corporeal miracles of our time,
transcending death and gender.

*Nach dtuigeann sibh,*[2] I rail infallibly,
that a priest in mortal need might nowadays
through benefit of after-death donation
be blessed to embrace and embody
a woman's eyes or heart,
kidneys, lungs or liver?

And conversely —
a resurrected woman
could be walking around
or making love while unaware
that her replacement vital organs
were endowed with Holy Orders?

---

[1] My shame on you, Pope, / (I lash out) fluently; / yourself and the old lads of
the Curia, / swanning around and hugger-muggering / in your fancy gowns of
purple or white / under Michelangelo's marvellous ceiling.
[2] Don't you understand?

*Ar aon nós, leanaim orm go rábach,*
*féach an chaoi a bhfuil cúrsaí*
*anseo i Ward B, Level 3,*
*i gcathair na long, ar bhruach' na Laoi:* [3]

There's Francesca from Milan
who watches over us all night,
calling out *arrivederci* in the morning
when she's going home
to see her son out to school
and get some sleep.

There's Alma from the Philippines
who checks on my incisions and courteously
inquires about my bowels.
(Once a month or so she gets through
to her husband and her daughter
at the house of an Irish priest
in the middle of the night
on the far side of the world.)

There's Imelda from Graunnabrahar
who does the morning obs
and deftly takes blood samples
though inconsolably in shock since
over-confident Cork hurlers
were dropped-on by Limerick
a week ago at Páirc Uí Chaoimh.

There's Geraldine from Cashel of the kings
who remakes beds and shines up floors
and empties all that must be emptied,

---

[3] In any case, I go on vociferously, / see how we're fixed down / here in Ward B, Level 3, / in the city of ships, on the banks of the Lee.

along with Sinéad and Marie
from Mitchelstown and Clonakilty
who carry in the meals,

and not forgetting Joan from Sundays Well
who later on will come round corridors and wards
with tinkling bell and veiled ciborium
of *panis angelicus*[4] on special offer.

*Éist, a Chearúil ró-ró-naofa,*[5]
surely no carnally conceived manjack
of the red-robed college would deny
*an taobh eile de leaba an tsaoil*
*go háirithe ó tharla é bheith*
*ó dhúchas chomh teolaí?*[6]

For isn't it one of the original mysteries
the way God's almighty divilment
saw fit to throw men and women
together in the world
in an eternal entanglement
of mutual mystification and delight,
torment and damnation,
succour and salvation?

These women here, *adeirim,*[7]
and others I could name
are no more Mícheálangelo angels
than you or me. They're just
as fabulously fallen, but in my book
they need no bishop's benediction
to be what they're already here —

---

[4] angelic bread. [5] Listen here, Karol, most most holy.
[6] the other side of the bed of life / especially since it's / so naturally cosy?
[7] I say.

*'sé sin le rá,*
*ina steille bheatha,*[8]
flesh-and-blood
priestesses.

Rome has weathered wild Gaels
from the west before. The old Pope
frowns and throws his eyes up
towards the Last Judgement.

He's stuck for words,
shackled to the *cúpla focal*[9]
drilled in by Ó Fiaich in '79.

*Dia dhuit,* he fences.
*Dia is Muire dhuit,* I point.
*Dia is Muire dhuit is Pádraig,* he parries.
*Dia is Muire dhuit is Pádraig agus Bríd —*[10]

I palpably hit home.

*Bíodh sin mar atá.*[11]
I've had my say in the Sistine Chapel
and wake up with the secret
satisfaction of a job well done,

the illusion that I've won.

---

[8] which is to say, / alive and kicking. [9] basic phrases.
[10] God be with you, (he fences). / God and Mary with you, (I point). / God,
Mary and Patrick, (he parries). / God and Mary, Patrick and Brigid —
[11] So let it be.

## Homo Erectus

*Bonjour*, Niamh,
flying home from France
and coming right on cue
to take my hand

this day
of my inaugural
wobble and re-entry
to the world of upright man.

Here you are,
helping me
with my first steps,

just as
twenty years ago
I did with yours.

## Recitals from the Cross

Richie is his own orchestra, rigged
and tuned to play recitals
from the cross of pain.

He's a heavy man, his speech
distorted by the tubing
and whatever is awry inside.

His mother comes each day
by bus from Bandon.
Only she knows what he tries to say

while she strokes his face for hours,
whispering Richie, oh Richie,
Richie, Richie.

The old woman doesn't eat all day,
then goes to catch the last bus home
leaving him her tears and her caresses

while he dozes for a while,
moaning like a sick whale
astray in the sea roads.

When he's bad it takes three nurses
to turn him and give him ease. One tries
to hurry down his medication.

Swallow it Richie, swallow, swallow,
you have to swallow it to get better.
Come on now Richie,
like a good boy, swallow.

Richie tries to do as he is told;
he makes the *molto agitato* music
of simultaneously swallowing
while throwing up.

One evening when his mother has gone
a young clergyman arrives
with a twang that twins
Nashville and Ballymena.

He finds the bed, checks
with the chart, intones
Ah Richard — it is Richard, yes?

So there you are.
I hear that you're
progressing.

Do you know some folks believe
the Lord sends suffering
to make us better?

Richie musters full
orchestral outrage,
starting with a roll of tympani
registering five
on the Richter Scale
from deep down
in the abdominal regions

and surfacing
with convulsive
groan and gurgle —

like a demented virtuoso
attempting Ludoveski's
*Cantata for Tuba* under water
while breathing through a pipe
inserted in his nose.

## Munster Aisling

On the day I'm going home
I wake at first light,
put earphones in place, turn on
Lyric and commune with Monteverdi,
immortally antiphonal across the universe.

And suddenly
out of brightening sky outside the window
a sense of Munster enters like an *aisling*[1]
and myself grounded in it, but uplifted,

*is Muimhneach mise*[2]
dawning on me

as though I'd just drunk some kind of potion
bringing me bright vision panning over
mountain ranges, river valleys, villages and towns,
places of poets, musicians, broken armies,
hunger and pestilence, bravery and beauty
holiness and slaughter, love and laughter
all the glens and hillsides, fields and streams
*ó Charraig na Siúire go ciumhais an Daingin siar*[3]

with, westward beyond last parishes,
vast kingdom of the wave presided over
by Manannáin Mac Lir, Poseidon,
sending untiring emissaries to challenge
Munster headlands, Slea and Beara
Kinsale, Ardmore, Helvic, and be appeased
and then seduced within their harbours —
entering the soft embrace
within the haven sound of *cuan*.[4]

---

[1] poetic vision: a genre of 18th-century poem/song. [2] I am of Munster.
[3] From Carrick-on-Suir westwards to the border of Dingle: quote from
'*Táim-se im' chodladh*', an 18th-century aisling song. [4] harbour.

Later in the morning I'm helped
to shower and shave and dress.
The whitecoated ones come round
to enquire, observe, appraise.

The surgeon listens to my heart,
which he held in his hands,
tells me about the healing process,
wishes me good health and creativity,
then takes time to talk of books.

He's from north Cork and knows
Elizabeth Bowen's resting place at Farrahy,
a place that I love for itself,
for the vanished great house
of Bowen's Court beside it,
and for all she wrote.

Before the summer ends I'll visit there again.
For now I quote to the white coats
her recognition of graveyards as
*places of returned innocence . . .*
*with something approaching gaiety in them.*

Such illumination exalts us all
on and in the earth, teaching us
to look upon it with love — this humbly
perfect earth we walk upon,
its patience with all woundings,
its unceasing restorations.

Lunchtime, and my wife arrives.
We pack my bits and pieces,
get well cards and medication,
with books that saw me through —

Heaney's effulgent *Electric Light*,
the salt storytelling of Alistair MacLeod —
along with items of Mediterranean magic
brought by pious friends from Italy:

a stone fragment from the cave
where St Michael was in the habit
of appearing, and a phial of holy oil,
*olio benedetto di San Mateo*,
from the shrine where thousands
flocked for centuries to revere
the upper apostolic molar (*primus
tricuspidus superioris*) of Matthew,
taxman and Evangelist, deceased.

At last I'm outside under open sky,
a fresh breeze on my face. Standing there
after my goodbyes and thanks,
I'm weak as water, but look back
in gratitude, discounting all shortcomings,
yea, even unto the Stalinist architecture.

By now my bed's remade
for yet another who needs care.
In there it's all still going on
and must continue — the unsung
and unceasing work of love,
in this place of hurt and healing,
grief and endings,
hope and new beginnings.

And inarticulate love is what I feel
as my wife drives me through the living
city streets, the radio announcing
that on this day in Ireland

the bones on tour
of St Thérèse of Liseux
are blocking traffic
in Derry of the siege.

We turn across the river and head east
beyond the city, through fields and villages
and towns, over the Blackwater, on past
Declan's well and bed and tower,
to the Famine graveyard of Reilig a' tSlé'
above Dungarvan Bay outspread in light,
then on under the Comeraghs, their high
and misted cliffs and corries

until we finally descend by soft hills
into lush lowlands of east Munster
and the valley of the Suir
the name of which means sister.

Here is my *cuan*,
where I began, and where I live,
this settlement of souls at the tide-head of the river,
all its living or lost hearts in place and time
under the abiding breast of Slievenamon.

As we cross the bridge I see
the tide is flooding.
Here I may grow strong,
begin again, be blessed, live on.

# Acknowledgements

Versions of some of the foregoing work were broadcast on RTE Radio 1 (*The Enchanted Way, Sunday Miscellany* and *The Open Mind*) and on RTE Lyric FM (*Quiet Quarter/Lyric Notes*) and published in *The Clifden Anthology* (ed. Brendan Flynn); *Full Tide* (Relay Books, Nenagh, 1999); *The Irish Times; The Living Stream: A Festschrift for Theo Dorgan* (Poetry Ireland, ed. Niamh Morris); *Natural Bridge* (University of Missouri-St Louis, guest ed. Eamonn Wall); *The Oxford Magazine* (poetry ed. Bernard O'Donoghue); *Podium* (ed. Noel King); *Poetry Ireland Review* (eds. Eva Bourke, Catherine Phil Mac Carthy, Maurice Harmon, Biddy Jenkinson, Mark Roper); *The SHOp* (ed. John and Hilary Wakeman); and *Southword* (Munster Literature Centre, ed. Patrick Galvin). The poem 'Thirteen Souls with Bread and Wine' was shortlisted in the Seacat Poetry Ireland National Poetry Competition, 2002.

My thanks for help and support in general and particular ways to Aosdána (An Chomhairle Ealaíon/The Arts Council); the poets Edward Power, Moya Cannon, Nuala Ní Dhomhnaill and Thomas McCarthy, and Michael Hartnett (still with us in spirit) and Michael's partner Angela Liston; to John Quinn, broadcaster and writer; Brendan Flynn and Clifden Community Arts; Jane and Gethin Griffiths, Abergwuan; Myles Pepper, Artswave, West Wales; Dave Caffrey, Allihies Language and Arts Centre, West Cork; Joe Kenny (Kenny PhotoGraphics), Fethard, County Tipperary; Tomás Ó Nialláin; Dick Casey; Nick Power; Steve Cleary; Bernie Cox; Bill Power; Bridget Kearney; Tommy Brett; Seán Aighleart; Rachel Finnegan; Siobhán and Seosamh Mac Ionmhain; Meanys Shoes; The Carraig Hotel; to my wife Martina and children Niamh, Lucy and James, and with particular gratitude to the following poets for their multi-lingual guest appearance here: Menna Elfyn (Ceredigion); James Fenton (County Antrim), Áine Uí Fhoghlú (County Waterford) and Rody Gorman (Isle of Skye).

I wish to thank John McGahern for permission to quote from his acclaimed novel *That They May Face the Rising Sun* (2002), and I record my deep gratitude to The Gallery Press and Jean and Peter Fallon for their encouragement and dedication.

Photographs, including copies of archival material, by the author.

While this book was going to press it was announced that in Spring 2004 Michael Coady will receive the eighth annual Lawrence O'Shaughnessy Award for Poetry of the University of St Thomas Centre for Irish Studies, St Paul, Minnesota.

*One Another* was launched by John Quinn at The Carraig Hotel, Carrick-on-Suir, on 14 December 2003.